DREAM PALACES
of Hollywood's Golden Age

By David Wallace

Photography by Juergen Nogai

Abrams, New York

Contents

Players

Scenes

Acknowledgments

This book is the result of immeasurable assistance from Richard Olsen, Dale Olson, Loretta Barrett, Nicholas Mullendore, and Marc Wanamaker. And all are indebted to the still lively ghosts of Hollywood who built these amazing relics of the film capital's golden age, as well as the farsighted individuals who restored them for a new century.

For Chris

Preface: **Hollywood**Restored

Interior designer Annie Kelly, co-owner of one of Hollywood's most fascinating homes, perfectly describes the allure of many houses built during the film capital's so-called golden age. "When I walk down the front steps of my house, I get goose bumps remembering that Greta Garbo often walked up and down the same steps," she says.

Such a nostalgic frisson isn't limited to the front steps of Kelly's home whose first tenants included the legendary M.G.M. costume designer Adrian and his soon-to-be wife, Janet Gaynor, winner of the first Best Actress Oscar™ in 1929. "We had a delicious dinner in the courtyard," recalled Mercedes de Acosta (Greta Garbo's lover) in her autobiography *Here Lies the Heart* (1960), "and he showed me his sketches for Greta's clothes [for the 1932 production of *Mata Hari*]. I suggested that she wear a long black cape for the scene at the end when she is shot." Well, it's not the same table in the courtyard today, but it *is* the same courtyard, essentially unchanged from that balmy night when Garbo, de Acosta, Adrian, and, presumably, Gaynor discussed the costumes Greta Garbo would wear in the film (the movie about the World War I spy costarring Lionel Barrymore and Ramon Novarro, which was not to be one of Garbo's best).

Kelly's home, shared with her husband, photographer Tim Street-Porter, is designed as a sort of Venetian pocket-palazzo, and a previous tenant named it "Villa

Frank Lloyd Wright's "Hollyhock House" was built for Aileen Barnsdall between 1919 and 1921. After years of neglect, the house is presently undergoing a foundation-to-roof restoration.

Vallombrosa" after a village in Tuscany. (More about this house appears on pp. 138–45). Such a theatrical aspect is common to many Hollywood homes and has always been part of the film capital's built environment. De Acosta continued in her book: "He [Adrian] was living on Whitley Heights and his house seemed more like a stage set than a residence, [with] all sorts of balconies which made it seem romantic and theatrical. But I felt it was as unreal as cardboard. I was not far wrong about this because one evening a large stone rolled down the mountain, broke through the wall of the house, and calmly set itself down in the living room, which could only happen in Hollywood."

When one recalls that many of the builders of Hollywood's most memorable residences spent their days designing, filming, or acting in make-believe settings, the appeal of a home that looks like a prop from a production of a Gilbert and Sullivan operetta is understandable. In fact, except for the boulder crashing through the wall, many of the houses and buildings celebrated in this book share the same sort of unreality. Which explains their attraction to people today.

Not all of them have survived. But enough have lived through indifference, neglect, fire, floods, and earthquakes to find a new, restored, or carefully preserved life for the new century in the hands of new owners.

Laurel Canyon's Fitzpatrick House (1936), by R.M. Schindler. Los Angeles based architect Jeff Fink completed an extensive restoration of the house in early 2005. While its new owners chose to retain most of the iconic building's original features, they did alter the kitchen.

But why restore? Until recently, no one much cared about houses from the golden age of Hollywood. "Hollyhock House," Frank Lloyd Wright's first—and now iconic—Los Angeles project built for Aline Barnsdall in 1920 was for years allowed to rot away by its owner, the City of Los Angeles, which allocated only $5,000 a year for continuing restoration and $2,000 a year to run the place. Now wiser heads have prevailed, and a major restoration is underway.

The reasons for restoration are as varied as the buildings themselves, but there is usually a hard choice over the cost of doing it well: does one bite the bullet and spend the money, time, and effort needed to restore an old classic, or hire a talented architect and build a new one? Some restore rather than demolish and rebuild because they love the old buildings. Some do it because older houses offer a more spacious living environment than many recently constructed homes. Some houses are considered historically important—especially those by architects such as Frank Lloyd Wright, Richard Neutra, and Rudolph Schindler—and often attract purists who refuse to even add air-conditioning when restoring them. Other owners, however, originally attracted by the aesthetic merits of a great house, justify making all sorts of changes in order to make the property "livable" today; such updating almost always includes new kitchens and bathrooms and, often, home theaters and swimming pools.

Modernist architect Richard Neutra designed Hollywood's famed Lovell House to be close to nature and filled with light.

Others restore classic homes for financial gain. One of the houses visited in this book was bought for $1.3 million in 1997 and restored for under a million dollars. In 2004 its owner estimated its market value at $10–$14 million. Even a home's accessories are sought after. Some years ago, a small sconce designed by Schindler for the Hollyhock House complex was offered at auction. (Under Wright's employment, Schindler supervised construction of Hollyhock and handled the designs of structures including Studio-Residence A, built in 1920.) It was in terrible shape and no one bought it. Offered recently at auction again, it sold for $25,000.

An early Frank Lloyd Wright house met a different fate: owned by the architecture department at the University of Southern California, Hollywood's Freeman House, built in 1924, today serves as a hands-on training lab for architecture students while the house undergoes restoration. However important a house may be, it may find no saviour. Despite its desperate condition, funds to restore Frank Lloyd Wright's celebrated Ennis-Brown House (1924) cannot be found.

Restoration can follow several routes. It can be scientifically based, but it also can be uninformed, willful, or even capricious. "The problem in restoration, at least a respectable restoration," says Brian Tichenor, whose Beverly Hills firm has done several multimillion dollar restorations in recent years, "is staying consistent with the

original architect's intent while acknowledging changing technologies and lifestyles." Such a philosophy is commendable, but extremely difficult to execute since the very building methods and building materials have changed dramatically in the last century. Tichenor adds: "So we aim to make as few obvious changes as possible. You try to get under the skin of the original architect and decide that if he had this [modern] stuff available, how would he [or she] have used it? I always try to take as much as possible from what was available at the time. Fixtures should be as close as possible to what was available and, if I can't find something, I fabricate it."

But, even with the mistakes some owners and developers make, many good things are being done. After years of neglect, the Hollywood sign—the worldwide symbol of the film capital as well as the industry that made it rich—was falling down in 1978, until a group of concerned citizens took it on themselves to save it. Since its restoration, the sign has reached such a global iconic status that even the late Pope John Paul II requested that his helicopter circle it when he visited Los Angeles in September 1987.

One of Hollywood's architectural tragedies is the fate of Frank Lloyd Wright's celebrated Ennis-Brown house. To date, funds have not been found to restore it.

An enlightened restoration: Hollywood's Cinerama Dome Theater is aesthetically and economically viable once again.

Today Hollywood is more protective of its storied past. Witness the careful preservation of the Cinerama Dome Theater (1963) designed by Welton Beckett Associates following the geodesic dome principles of Buckminster Fuller and one of only a few remaining in the country; the general cleaning up of Hollywood Boulevard to rid it of sleazy tattoo parlors and sidewalk drug dealers; and the multimillion dollar restoration of Hollywood's neon signs, once celebrated in film and writings as the true symbol of Hollywood. This book is a celebration of that new spirit, which is not limited to the boundaries of Hollywood itself. The spirit of preserving both the great and humble homes from the film industry's storied past has spread throughout the Los Angeles basin, from downtown to Pacific Palisades to Malibu. The greater Hollywood, if you will.

The best reason for the restoration of Hollywood's golden age buildings is, as the owner of the Adrian House suggests, that by their very presence, they can transport us back to that fabled time. And isn't conveying us to another place and another time the ultimate purpose of the movies themselves?

Players

BeeryResidence

Above: Wallace Beery, one of the most beloved character actors of Hollywood's golden age, owned three homes. Here he is shown at his Beverly Hills mansion.

In 1936, residential architect William Kesling, a native of Texas, was Los Angeles's most successful practitioner of the popular Streamline Moderne style. According to Kesling authority Patrick Pascal, of the thirty-one houses designed by Kesling Modern Structures, a unique firm that handled both the design and construction of its buildings, only eighteen remain. Of those, six have been disfigured beyond repair by subsequent remodeling. Among the extant Keslings is an 1800-square-foot jewel in Hollywood that is considered one of the area's great examples of the Streamline Moderne house.

Kesling designed the home for the famous character actor Wallace Beery in 1936, and it cost only $3,500, about the average for an ordinary home at the time. Beery, who owned a Spanish Colonial Revival-style home in Beverly Hills, became so enamored by the Kesling look that he ordered two houses—this one and a nearby duplex—for sites located twelve blocks from Goldwyn Studio, where he was under contract.

Born in 1889 in Kansas City, Missouri, Beery began his entertainment career as a circus performer and vaudeville juggler. In 1916, after doing musical comedy on Broadway, he appeared with Gloria Swanson in a couple of one-reel comedies made at Essenay Studios (In one Beery appeared in drag as a Swedish housemaid). Although Beery went on to be known for tough-guy roles in gangster movies, in 1930 he was cast against type in *Min and Bill*, a film which also starred Marie Dreiser. It placed Beery among Hollywood's most loved actors. The following year, Beery won an Oscar for his role in *The Champ*, the ultimate four-hanky film. In it he costarred with the young Jackie Cooper.

Beery was also known for having a problem with alcohol, however, and he did a lot of partying in his Streamline Moderne house. In 1949, he died of a heart attack.

In 1980, the Beery House was bought by David and Maddie Sadofsky, owners of Hollywood's nostalgia store "Thanks for the Memories," and, with input from a Beery descendant and an actress who had appeared with him in some Spanish language films, they set out to restore the house to its former glory. It was a daunting task.

The floors were so dirty that your feet would stick to it. "The fireplace [constructed of a beige Roman brick] had been painted with dark brown enamel," Maddie Sadofsky says, "and then covered with a sort of chalet-style wrought iron framework that extended five feet out into the room. One of the living room walls was painted gold and the others covered with alternating, four-foot-wide panels of gold-veined mirrors and imitation-wood paneling." The living room floor was covered with a "hideous" green shag carpet; Kesling's soaring windows, a staple of his Moderne homes, were covered with filthy olive green drapes; and, in the middle of the ten-foot-high ceiling, was hung a wagon wheel chandelier.

The plumbing was upgraded to copper, and throughout the house, wide wood Venetian blinds were hung to provide privacy. The narrow kitchen was completely revamped to gain six inches of width. Today, a countertop range sits

Unlike most homes that show off their entrances, architect Kesling hid the entrance to the Wallace Beery home. It is located to the left, around the corner of the house and opposite the fountain.

on the black-and-red tile that replaced the original (and unobtainable) pale yellow and persimmon colored tiles. Still intact in the back hall under the era's ubiquitous closet ironing board, is a cunning brass frame for mounting a shoe to be polished.

"We did it in stages," the Sadofskys recall, "and it took about two years." The floors were stripped and refinished, and the tile in the bath, which had been painted aluminum, was ripped out and replaced with black and green tile—the green chosen because it closely matched the hue of 1930s green. The Streamline Moderne horizontal "speed lines" on the house and the shade-blocker arch (it once opened onto an avocado grove) in the backyard, which resembles a relic from an Art Deco gasoline station, were highlighted in a dark grayish-green hue that the couple matched to a Bauerware plate, a line of pottery popular in California in the 1930s. Later it was recognized to be an exact match with the Ford Motor Company's "Dartmouth Green" color that was popular on its cars in 1939.

Like many of Frank Lloyd Wright's houses, the flat roofs of the Kesling Moderne houses leaked badly. The problem was finally solved by the new owner, a screenwriter named Michael Taylor who bought the house in 1997, with the availability of a new, rubberized roofing material.

"Unlike other modernists," says Pascal of Kesling, "he was more relaxed. He may have felt 'Hey, this is Hollywood! Let's have fun.'"

A Streamline Moderne "shade blocker" arch separates the house from the back yard, originally an avocado grove.

Left: The green and black tiles in the restored bathroom were chosen to closely match a popular style of the 1930s.

Master bedroom of the Beery house. The wide wooden Venetian blinds and cabinetry were added by the present owner.

Opposite: The Wallace Beery home viewed from the backyard—the one-time avocado grove.

DeMilleHouse

Opposite: The entrance to the
Charles Chaplin house. It was
restored in the early 1990s and
modified somewhat since.

Cecil B. DeMille and his
secretary in 1923.

For years it has been said in Hollywood that the first thing an actor does after he or she becomes successful is to buy an expensive house. Then maybe you bought a flashy car, and then, at least in Hollywood's golden age, you probably bought a yacht. Among the first to do it all was the legendary director Cecil B. DeMille.

In 1916, with his fame growing fast, DeMille bought one of the two houses built next to each other to launch an exclusive Hollywood development called Laughlin Park. He then bought a racy Locomobile roadster (a car then as famous—and as expensive—as a Rolls Royce is today), and a 106-foot sailing yacht, *The Seaward*.

The house next door to DeMille's, designed by a local architect named Clarence Dodd, was rented by a man who was already the most famous star in the world, Charlie Chaplin. Then, after Chaplin moved in 1917, DeMille bought the house to serve as a 5,000-square-foot home office.

Top: Charles Chaplin, ca. 1916. DeMille's office often served as an informal screening room.

DeMille's wife, Constance, was responsible for furnishing and running the first house and saw to it that heads of state and industry leaders were entertained royally. But it was from his office in the second house that, for more than forty years until his death in 1959, the director exercised his power and prerogatives as the uncrowned king of Hollywood. Occasionally, he even used the property as a location; a scene from his famous 1927 film *King of Kings* was shot in an olive grove on the grounds.

Walking into the beautifully restored living room of that house is a spine-tingling experience. There, in the large bay with its leaded glass windows, where a pair of comfortable chairs now sit, was the desk where DeMille developed most of his seventy films that are part of Hollywood history: *The Ten Commandments* (both the 1923 film and its 1956 remake, which would be DeMille's final film); 1934's *Cleopatra* with Claudette Colbert; *Union Pacific* (1939); *Unconquered* (1947); and 1952's *The Greatest Show on Earth*, the only film for which he won an Oscar™. From that desk, the director could gaze at his countless awards and Oscar™ displayed atop a large built-in bookcase, filled with history books like H.G. Wells's *History of the World*. For years after his death in January 1959, his secretary, who came in daily to attend to family business, would make certain that the desk calendar was turned to the proper date and that all the pencils were sharpened.

Today the desk and the bookcase are gone, but the bookcase remains in spirit. The original intricately carved mahogany columns that once defined its design have been integrated into a mahogany cabinet that hides modern electronics. But it was nearly lost. "When the previous owners bought it in the mid-1990s," says the present owner (appropriately a film and television producer), who acquired the property in 1999, "it was in such bad repair they thought seriously of razing the house . . . there were actually coyotes living in the attic."

Opposite: The living room, originally DeMille's office.

All that remained of the original stairwell prior to restoration were pieces of the mahogany paneling and rail.

Opposite: The home's spacious kitchen was created from several smaller rooms during the restoration and renovation.

Brian Tichenor, who, with his wife, runs Tichenor and Thorp, a Beverly Hills landscape and building architectural firm, spent the next eighteen months heading up a multimillion dollar restoration of the house. "The place was in very, very bad shape," Tichenor says, "totally dilapidated... Actually words cannot describe how horrible it was. The only thing that was livable was the living room (DeMille's office) which also served as a screening room, the rest of the place was nothing. In a day when home theater is a multibillion dollar industry, it comes as a bit of a shock that a 'screening room' in the early days was nothing more or less than a projector and a screen set up wherever you were—like showing movies in a fourth-grade class today."

During the DeMille era, the director used the entire upstairs, a rabbit warren of small rooms, to store his papers; accordingly, Tichenor's biggest challenge—more than clearing out the coyotes and cleaning the place up—"was to make the house coherent." In addition to major work on the upstairs—during which a large, open master bedroom was created—a kitchen had to be carved out of several small rooms on the main floor. In the basement that was undeveloped, a maid's room and gym were built. The mahogany-paneled stairwell was also in pieces, but luckily, there was enough left to copy for the restoration.

Because the breezeway that connected the DeMille residence next door and the house that served as his office had largely rotted away, it was removed. Tichenor came up against the frequently told story that the breezeway had been designed by the Bay Area architect Julia Morgan, famed for designing publisher William Randolph Hearst's San Simeon estate as well as his *Examiner* building in Los Angeles. "I went

Opposite: The master bedroom
of the house was carved out
of several smaller rooms during
restoration and renovation.
The present owners added
the bookcase to hide a back
staircase.

The intricate marble mosaic
design on the master bathroom's
floor was recently added by the
present owner.

into the matter thoroughly," Tichenor says, "and it turns out that there is absolutely no evidence that she had anything to do with the design of the breezeway except that there is a record that she visited DeMille at one point and that some of the window treatments in what is left of the breezeway look something like her work in the Bay Area. She may have made a sketch on a napkin or something which DeMille could have given to a contractor." It is fairly certain, however, that Frank Lloyd Wright, Jr. (known as Lloyd) designed the leaded glass windows of the solarium off the living room and the front door of the house.

The film vault where DeMille stored his films was also beyond repair. The rebar reinforcement of the concrete structure had corroded and the roof had collapsed. It has been replaced with a greenhouse in which the present owner raises orchids. Tichenor also put in the new pool and gardens, and hired art restorers to replicate the wall decoration of the loggia from old photographs. He put a new roof on the house to which he later added solar panels for heating water.

"The house was mostly restored when we bought it," says the new owner. "We completed the landscaping and some exterior hardscaping." The previous owners made two larger bedrooms out of the four upstairs. Because the bathrooms remained small, however, the new owners decided to move a closet into the sitting room off the master bedroom and enlarge the master bathroom to its present luxurious dimensions. The house no longer has the same floor plan, but thanks to a meticulous, historically respectful restoration, it does have the spirit of that time when Hollywood ruled world entertainment, and Cecil B. DeMille ruled Hollywood.

From what is now a playroom off the living room, a breezeway once connected the house to DeMille's next door residence.

Opposite: An olive grove near the new swimming pool served as a location for DeMille's 1927 film *King of Kings*.

DohenyResidence

Opposite: The rambling Doheny mansion near downtown Los Angeles. Built in 1899, it first received a major restoration following the devasting Long Beach earthquake of 1933.

Estelle Doheny (left) and her sister Daysie Mae Anderson in the mansion's giant (and long vanished) greenhouse, ca. 1950.

Great architecture and historical importance can define a house for future generations. Homes can also be made famous by their residents. Such is the case for the lavish house built in 1899 on Chester Place near downtown Los Angeles, then a fashionable area for millionaires. It was bought in 1901 by Edward L. Doheny and his wife, Estelle, and is one of Los Angeles's most remarkable homes. Its most prominent resident became rich and famous for pioneering the area's oil industry, which, in turn, provided much of the funds for the growth of the film industry. He was also notorious for precipitating the greatest U.S. government scandal before Watergate. He and his wife also endured a personal tragedy and erected two grand buildings that remain, more than seventy-five years later, among the city's proudest showpieces.

The house was designed by the firm of Theodore Eisen and Sumner Hunt in an eclectic style, which they called "Gothic Renaissance," for the Oliver P. Posey family. Despite Sumner Hunt's

reputation as one of the city's most eminent architects (he would later design the Southwest Museum, one of the earliest examples of Mission Revival architecture), the *Los Angeles Times* was unconvinced. The paper described its combination of French château, Gothic, English Tudor, and even California Mission architectural styles as one "heretofore of doubtful congruity." The interior was originally as eclectic as the exterior. The present Great Hall was done as a Tudor/Gothic hunting lodge complete with stuffed game and bear skins cohabiting with cherubs. In 1906, by enclosing an octagonal courtyard, designer A. F. Rosenheim added what is today the mansion's most spectacular attribute: the so-called Pompeiian Room. Capped by a spectacular, forty-foot dome constructed of Tiffany gold-favrile glass, the room remains an elegant combination of marble, glass, and gold suitable for lavish entertainment. Despite the name, "Pompeiian" elements are few. The home's curator, MaryAnn Bonino, explains: "They're largely a matter of fantasy or allusion via Wedgewood-style medallions lining the gold-leaf and bronze-accented walls of this quasi-atrium. The marble columns and geometrically patterned floor, for instance, are more neo-Classical than Pompeiian and, although the Pompeiian-red upholstery on the chairs was copied from designs in Rome's National Museum, the chair frames are French Empire." At the same time as the Pompeiian Room was added, Mrs. Doheny built a small zoo housing deer, rare birds, and monkeys, and a bowling alley (called "Wigwam") for her husband and his friends.

Because the 2,836 glass leaves of the Pompeiian Room's dome were loosely mounted in their metal-alloy frames, all have survived numerous earthquakes. The house itself suffered serious structural damage in the Long Beach earthquake in 1933. Afterward, the couple called in the famous architect Wallace Neff, and designer Horace Mann, to reinforce and redecorate the house. They replaced much

The Doheny's often entertained political and Roman Catholic hierarchy in the huge dining room.

of the original timber construction with steel, and the cherubs won the decorating debate. The interior oak pillars were replaced with marble columns topped with Corinthian capitals; ceilings were molded in Rococo detail picked out in gold leaf, and eighteenth-century French furniture was favored in the first-floor formal rooms. The music room shelters a rare 1925 French piano, played as recently as 1986 by the famed pianist Alicia De Larrocha. Her appearance was part of Los Angeles's highly praised Chamber Music in Historic Sites series, which, under the auspices of the Da Camera Society of Mount St. Mary's College, presents several concerts annually in the mansion.

In 1892, Doheny was probably the first person to discover oil in Los Angeles when he noticed seepage near today's intersection of Beverly and Glendale Boulevards in the Echo Park community. By the time he bought the house on Chester Place, he was well on his way to becoming America's first "oillionaire," buying leases wherever he could and exploring for oil reserves in both California and Mexico. By the early 1920s his eighty-one wells were producing an annual income of $10 million, and he scented more money at a site called Elk Hills in Kern County, some one hundred miles north of Los Angeles. A few years before, 80,000 acres of proven oil fields at the site had been placed in reserve for the future needs of the U.S. Navy. Doheny convinced President Harding's Secretaries of the Navy and Interior that the oil was being siphoned off by neighboring drillers, and claimed that if the leases were transferred to Doheny's company, such theft would be stopped. To close the deal, Doheny had his son, Edward Jr., accompanied by his secretary, Hugh Plunkett, deliver a suitcase containing $100,000 to the Interior Secretary, Albert Fall. Fall, however, insisted on transferring navy oil reserves in Wyoming to oilman Harry Sinclair (who had also bribed Fall with $400,000 and livestock for his New Mexico ranch). The resulting scandal became known by the name of those Wyoming oil reserves: Teapot Dome.

Opposite: The centerpiece of the mansion's music room is a rare 1925 Pleyel piano, which Mrs. Doheny imported from Paris.

Left: The showpiece of the
mansion is the Pompeiian
Room, added in 1906.

A pair of sphinxes bear silent
witness to the dramatic history
of the Doheny mansion.

The Pompeiian Room's 40-foot gold-glass dome is made of more than 2,800 leaves of gold-colored Tiffany glass.

It all came to light in 1923 when Fall, presumably because he knew the scheme was about to explode, retired. Then, in August of that year, President Harding died and was succeeded by Calvin Coolidge. An investigation of the lease transfers began. Eventually Fall was convicted of accepting a bribe but Doheny, thanks to a defense that cost him $15 million in today's money, was acquitted.

This episode led Doheny to suggest a movie plot. As Cecil B. DeMille recalls in his autobiography: "It was a few years after the so-called 'oil scandals' of the Harding administration, but while they were still fresh in public memory, that Edward L. Doheny invited me to lunch one day. He wanted, he said, to discuss a possible subject for a motion picture." During the lunch, Doheny suggested that DeMille make a movie that would give Doheny's side of the Teapot Dome story. DeMille added: "It would have made [a good movie and] one of the most talked of motion pictures of the decade. But the New York executives thought that it was too political and controversial; so it joined the list of pictures that were never made."

About the time that the scandal broke, the Dohenys had embarked on a rarely matched campaign of philanthropy. In 1924 they commissioned architect Albert C. Martin to design and build the grand St. Vincent de Paul Catholic church near their estate; inspired by eighteenth-century Mexican baroque architecture, it remains one of the city's architectural gems. After their son and Hugh Plunkett died in 1929, under mysterious circumstances in Greystone—the 47,000-square-foot Tudor mansion they had built for him the previous year—the couple built the Edward L. Doheny Jr. Library at the nearby University of Southern California as a memorial.

Doheny died in 1935, and, following Mrs. Doheny's death in 1958, the residence—and the entire Chester Place complex—passed to the Roman Catholic archdiocese. Soon after, it became the downtown campus of Mount St. Mary's College, which, acting as a steward of the mansion, uses it for special events and is embarking on a campaign for its conservation.

DurantResidence

It was a marriage that scandalized many in 1913: he was a twenty-eight-year-old teacher, she was a fifteen-year-old student of his at New York's experimental libertarian Ferrer Modern School. She roller-skated to their wedding at City Hall.

In Hollywood, where the length of marriages seems to be weeks or months, the couple went on to make history by remaining happily married for sixty-eight years before dying two weeks apart in 1981. Along the way, they made history another way, by collaborating for many of the fifty years it took to write what was then—and remains—the most comprehensive and popular history of humankind, the eleven-volume *The Story of Civilization*. They are Will and Ariel Durant, whose memory is celebrated by a new branch library in Hollywood. *The Story of Civilization* together with his 1926 epic *Story of Philosophy* (which launched the success of Simon & Schuster), sold more than seventeen million copies. This memory is very much alive in the recently restored "Casa della Vista," in

Opposite: This 1920s Hollywood Hills estate was home to historians Will and Ariel Durant for 38 years.

Hollywood, so named by the couple for its sweeping views of Los Angeles. It was their home for thirty-eight years.

After completing the first three volumes of *The Story of Civilization*, Will and Ariel (whom he nicknamed "Puck" before their marriage), moved with their daughter, Eleanor, from their home in Great Neck on Long Island to Hollywood. There, Jim Fifield, an old friend of Will's and pastor of the First Congregational Church in Los Angeles, helped the couple find a house in the Hollywood Hills. The one they bought was a massive structure built as speculation on Briarcliff Road in the mid-1920s, which, like many others in the city, had been abandoned by the previous resident out of fear that the Japanese would soon be marching up Hollywood Boulevard. The house was (and is) a fascinating blend of the earlier Craftsman style with the Spanish Colonial Revival style, but it was in terrible shape. "The building had been neglected, with broken windows welcoming the rain [and] was surrounded by weeds taller than men," Durant recalled in 1980. "We bought the ruin, repaired it, have lived in it contentedly now for thirty-seven years."

During those years, the busy couple came up with a *modus vivendi* that allowed them to both research and write *The Story of Civilization*. Ariel would rise early and go downstairs. A little later, the dapperly dressed Will would stride down the dramatic entrance-hall stair for his whole-wheat bread and grapefruit breakfast. Besides organizing Will's life, Ariel also organized much of his research. While he wrote upstairs she worked downstairs, spreading scraps of colored paper containing Will's thoughts on the current book project across the table in the large oval dining room. Durant averaged five years producing each volume of *Civilization*; three years were devoted to researching the era in question, and two years to writing. That dining room table was also the centerpiece around which the highly social Durants entertained the likes of Albert Einstein, Charlie Chaplin, and Errol Flynn.

On a table in the home's oval dining room, Ariel Durant once laid out research notes for *The Story of Civilization.*

As part of his 1980 thoughts about their house, Will Durant added: "And [we] pray for the privilege of dying there whenever the Reaper finds us fit for remolding." Their prayer was answered when Will was admitted to the hospital with heart problems at the age of ninety-six. Ariel, fearing that he would not be returning to their home, stopped eating and died on October 25. On November 7, Will's own heart stopped beating. "We could do almost anything if time would slow up," the philosopher/historian once remarked, "but time runs on, and we melt away trying to keep up with it."

The Story of Civilization is out of print, and, following the deaths of the Durants, their "Casa della Vista" faced neglect. When it was sold a year after the couple's death, the grounds where Ariel would garden daily looked abandoned, and raccoons riddled the house where paint was peeling from the walls. The new owners had the raccoons trapped and shipped off to a wildlife station in the San Fernando Valley, cleared out hundreds of boxes of books from the tower room where Durant wrote, and threw away thousands of foreign language editions of *The Story of Civilization* stored in the garage.

The new owners found long forgotten tilework by lauded design theorist and artisan Ernest Batchelder under the grime covering the fireplace and fountain, and, under wall-to-wall carpeting, marble and tile floors. The easiest part of the restoration was replacing many broken leaded glass windows, the most difficult was sandblasting the exterior, and stripping down the spouts and wrought-iron trim.

Although the house returned to livable condition, aesthetic deterioration continued. A subsequent owner painted all the wrought iron in the interior bright gold, and the original tiles in the master bath were replaced with bright red ones. The next owner then covered all of the downstairs walls with a rough finish that "looked like frosting on

a supermarket cake," according to one visitor, "some of the peaks were an inch high; you could get hurt brushing against it."

In 1999, the house was bought by film producers Keith Addis and his wife, Keri Selig, who embarked on a meticulous ten-month restoration. "The challenge was to make the house comfortable on a contemporary level without destroying its style," Addis says. He adds that the concept of the house was an idealized version of what they suspected the 1940s film star Veronica Lake (whose portrait hangs in an upstairs hall) would have done if she had had the money and the opportunity.

One of the first things they did was to lower a video camera down the chimneys. "They are the spinal cord of a house," Addis explains, "and are the ultimate historical archive of earthquake damage." Happily no damage was found, because, according to Addis, the house is built on solid granite, covered with twelve inches of topsoil. "That gives it great stability," he adds, "but it's a bad gardening issue." When the couple bought the house, they found that the lawn was gone and the many trees on the two-acre property "were in major need of resuscitation." Today the lawn has been restored to a parklike ambiance and is enhanced by orange, plum, avocado, fig, and pomegranate trees. Roses, many planted in a collection of 1930s and 1940s pots, bloom profusely.

Inside, the cake-frosting plaster in the downstairs rooms was removed and the walls were finished smooth. Every wire and pipe in the house was replaced, and four new bathrooms replaced the aged originals, but all were designed in the style of the early 1920s. One major change was the addition of a large outdoor dining gazebo on an overlook bluff about a hundred feet from the house. Aside from new cooking appliances in the gazebo, its style and period color match the house perfectly; with Hollywood's climate, it has become the couple's favorite site for dining and entertaining. Other than replacing the plastic cabinet windows with reeded glass, little needed to be done in the kitchen, which had been restored in an era-friendly style by the

Opposite: A recent addition to the site is this outdoor gazebo, built in the 1920s style of the house.

During restoration and renovation, the sills of the windows of the west-facing master bedroom were lowered so that the owners could enjoy the view from their bed.

Oppposite: The west facade
of the house. Will Durant wrote
most of *The Story of Civilization*
on the top room of the tower.

The master bathroom, which
is in the tower.

previous owners. The current owners of the house restored and modernized the
Durants' original tennis court.

The successful result of another modification is especially gratifying to Addis.
When built, the sills of the windows in the tower aerie where Durant wrote were
so high off the floor that, when seated, one couldn't enjoy the spectacular view.
Replacing them with windows that reached closer to the floor seemed impossible as
all the windows were curved to match the shape of the tower. Through his contractor,
Addis located the only company in Southern California still making curved glass and
the resulting windows look like they have been there always. "I work up there every
night," Addis says. "And from my desk I now can enjoy the sensational view of the
city. I love the sound of the Hollywood freeway," which snakes through the hills far
below the house. "It's like a river. And at night, with all the traffic, it looks like a long
neon sign."

In 1986, five years after the Durants' death and a year after the death of their
daughter, their granddaughter found, in a stash of shoe boxes, love letters her grand-
parents had exchanged three-quarters of a century before. Today, thanks to a loving
restoration, the home where Will and Ariel Durant lived joins those letters in keeping
alive the memory of one of Hollywood's greatest literary collaborations—and love
stories.

W.C.FieldsResidence

Opposite: The house that was once home to W.C. Fields was built in Hollywood's Laughlin Park enclave in 1919 and restored in 1999–2000.

W.C. Fields and friends at the lily pond.

It's not exactly news that many film and television stars are somewhat lacking good judgment, especially when it comes to the decoration of their homes. It has been this way since Hollywood began a century or so ago. Errol Flynn, for example, built a New England cottage in the Hollywood hills in the 1930s. Such a house was incongruous and inappropriate in Southern California, but understandable; it was "comfortable" architecture. Few actors of the 1930s were adventurous enough to opt for the now-classic cutting-edge designs of Richard Neutra or Rudolph Schindler. What really set Flynn's house apart, though, was the interior decoration which, among other things, included a one-way mirror so he and his friends could view couples copulating in the guest bedroom and an aquarium in the den, which was backed with an obscene mural. But at least he kept the place in good repair.

You couldn't say the same about a famous mansion built in 1919 in Hollywood's upscale Laughlin Park enclave; to survive, it not only

The dramatic entrance is
surmounted by a stained-
glass window.

had to overcome deliberate neglect in the late 1930s, but astonishingly wrong-headed decoration in the 1980s by one of America's most celebrated comediennes.

Usually referred to as the W.C. Fields House, the five-bedroom, five-bath, 6,400-square-foot house was designed by an architect named Clarke (nothing else is known of him) for oilman Frank Wood and his wife. It was planned to showcase what seems like acres of antique mahogany paneling the couple bought from a Spanish monastery. This paneling was very important to the Woods, because to acquire it the couple had to outbid publisher William Randolph Hearst, then one of America's richest men, who was shopping in Europe at the time for furnishings for his legendary San Simeon estate. The Woods' house cost $20,300 to build in an era when the average house could be erected for perhaps $3,000.

Eventually the Woods rented it to Maurice Chevalier, and later to Paramount producer William LeBaron. W.C. Fields was one of Hollywood's most famous actors (as well as curmudgeons) and LeBaron was his self-proclaimed biggest fan and producer of many of his films, including 1934's *It's A Gift*. Fields wanted LeBaron's house so much that, on one occasion when the producer was desperately ill, Fields repeatedly called the hospital hoping to be told that the producer had died. "I don't think Bill actually wanted me to die," LeBaron said afterwards. "But he was a practical man, and he sure planned to get that house if I did die. As it turned out, I moved and he got it anyway."

W.C. Fields, also known as one of Hollywood's great drinkers, rented the place in 1940 for $250 a month. (Fields always rented, preferring to hide his wealth in dozens of savings accounts.) The rent included the services of a Japanese gardener for the two-thirds-acre property reportedly landscaped by Frank Lloyd Wright's son, Lloyd, a famous architect in his own right. Fields lived in this house when he made most of his more familiar films, including 1940's *The Bank Dick* and *My Little Chickadee*. He lived there until he moved to the sanitarium where "The Man in the

Entrance hall of the mansion. During parties, Fields would often hide behind the small grille-covered window (left, center) to eavesdrop on guests.

The master bedroom. When the house was restored, central air conditioning and heating were added throughout.

Bright Nightgown"—Fields's phrase for death—called for him on Christmas Day, 1946. According to his long-time mistress, Carlotta Monti, he loved this house more than any other place he called home.

One wouldn't know that from the way he took care of the place. When Fields rented it, he was one of the few Americans who had money to throw around; in fact, he used to wander about the house in a white terry-cloth bathrobe, one pocket filled with a thick roll of money, the other with more than thirty keys to the double-locked cabinets and trunks where he stored his liquor and beer. When the economy improved, the Woods wanted to raise the rent and offered to renovate the place. Fields was incensed. "All landlords should get the electric chair," he said to his friend, journalist Gene Fowler. "Let the joint fall apart." And that, more or less, is what happened.

According to Fowler, the place became so run down it took on the appearance of Poe's House of Usher. "Where the wallpaper had not fallen off, it hung like tattered battle standards," Fowler recalled in his book *Minutes of the Last Meeting* (1954). He added that most of the rugs were threadbare, and chunks of plaster would often fall down on the pool table making play somewhat hazardous (the pool table and a min-iature bowling alley were two of Fields's few contributions to the home's furnishings).

In another room Fields installed a barber's chair so he could have his hair cut at home; in those days that cost fifty cents less. Upstairs, Fields built one of Hollywood's first exercise rooms, complete with rowing machine, stationary bicycle, steam cabinet, and, several times weekly, a personal trainer named Bob Howard (whose clients included Cole Porter, Myrna Loy, and Irving Berlin). Fields, who often made fun of his very serious drinking, loved his rowing machine and would place a drink two feet from the rear of the device. Then, rowing desperately, he would pretend to chase it. "I'm gaining," he once shouted at Howard. "These workouts are going to increase my liquor consumption [by] two or three hundred percent!"

Fields didn't think much more of Hollywood than he did of landlords. He once commented, "I've been asked if I ever get the d.t.'s. I don't know, it's hard to tell where

Hollywood ends and the d.t.'s begin." Not surprisingly, one imperative addition to the house was the installation of three bars. These were supplemented by a portable bar made from a child's wagon and an old icebox so refreshment would be handy, according to Fowler, in case Fields got thirsty walking through a hallway. There was also another bar in the trailer in which he, Fowler, and John Barrymore used to travel to prizefights, and there was a refrigerated bar bolted to the floorboards of his V-16 Cadillac (now in the collection of Las Vegas's Imperial Palace Hotel, *sans* bar and his famous electric martini mixer). He was perhaps proudest of his expensive sound system to spy on his servants, with microphones hidden in chandeliers, behind pictures, and under tables and chairs.

Another addition of "Uncle Claude's" (as his friends called him—he was born William Claude Dukenfield) resulted in one of the famous tragedies of the era. In January 1941, his secretary, Magda Michael, gave him a model boat, presumably for his sixty-first birthday, and he put it in the lily pond on the property. On March 15, 1941, while producer Cecil B. DeMille's daughter and her husband, Anthony Quinn, were visiting her father and mother across the street, the couple's three-year-old son Christopher wandered over to Fields's property. There, apparently attracted by the toy boat, the child fell in the pond and drowned.

The next day Fields burned the boat in his incinerator, drained the water from the pond, and never went near the site again. Nevertheless, his eccentricity remained as strong as ever. For one thing, he kept a rifle handy in case any "hairy-nosed wombats," presumably from the nearby Griffith Park Zoo, wandered onto his doorstep, and often threatened to shoot his neighbor, the singing actress Deanna Durbin, because he couldn't stand hearing her voice when she was practicing. One time during World War II, he shot at the local air raid warden patrolling the neighborhood in the dark; it was Mr. DeMille—a man he hated both because of his power and because DeMille's house sat on higher land than his own. In any event, DeMille was so rattled by the experience that he thereafter assigned his butler to make the nightly rounds.

After Fields gave up the house, the Woods sold it to the Australian-born actress Ann Richards and her producer/director husband Edward Angelo whose family lived there for nearly a quarter century. Richards made few films, but among them was a costarring role in 1948's Barbara Stanwyck/Burt Lancaster film *Sorry Wrong Number.* Her son recalls that when he and his friends were growing up, they would sometimes find old cigar butts—Fields loved his stogies—tucked away in odd corners of the basement. In 1972 they sold the house to a psychiatrist who sold it in 1978 to comedienne Lily Tomlin and her partner and collaborator Jane Wagner. Eccentricity returned with a vengeance.

The shallow cabinets they installed near the front door were not particularly intrusive; they were put there so Tomlin could stash her eyeglasses. But it was odd, to say the least, to paint everything—inside and outside the house—Pepto-Bismol pink. It was also expensive to remove.

When the next tenants, an entertainment industry couple, acquired the place in 1999, their task was laid out for them. Aided as they were with the original plan of the house, it still took four years and reportedly well over a million dollars to return the place to its former glory. To remove that pink paint from the antique paneling took nine workmen over three months; sometimes they were forced to work with toothbrushes so as not to damage the intricate carved details. Vintage and reproduction fixtures were found and installed to replace inappropriate accessories added to the house in later years. In addition, the pool and landscaping were renovated, a number of century-old dwarf olive trees were planted, the kitchen was renovated, and a new unobtrusive family room was added. During this time, the new owners lived in one of Fields's liquor storage areas in the basement. Today the house gleams with fresh life—from the paneling to the small, grille-covered window through which Fields, seated in a closet, would eavesdrop on the conversations of his guests partying in the mansion's front hall/ballroom.

In 2003 the house was resold to Dennis Rice, a Disney executive and his wife, Monique, who are dedicated to preserving the charm of the house well into the new century.

Grant/**Scott**Residence

Opposite: The first home of
Cary Grant and Randolph Scott,
built in 1926. It was completely
restored in the mid-1990s.

Cary Grant at home.

If Cary Grant is not the most celebrated male movie star of Hollywood's golden age, he's pretty close to it. His elegant, urbane
screen persona became a classic from the days when he played the
straight man (more about that later) opposite Mae West in 1933's
I'm No Angel and *She Done Him Wrong* (in which she seductively
invited Grant—in one of her most famous quotes—to "come up
sometime and visit me"). Before long it would be Grant's movies that
were the classics, such as Howard Hawks's 1940 screwball comedy
His Girl Friday (costarring Rosalind Russell), and Hitchcock's 1959
masterpiece *North by Northwest.*

Today, when it's popular to deconstruct reputations and tradi-
tions, it is little wonder that Grant's sexual orientation is openly
debated. Despite five marriages, it has become clear that, if not gay,
he was probably bisexual. In 1932 the twenty-eight-year-old Archie
Leach first arrived in Hollywood (his screen name came soon after
when he signed a five-year contract with Paramount), and for many

Entrance to the Grant/Scott
home in the Hollywood Hills.

Opposite: The entrance hall
of the house boasts an unusal
stained-glass window.

years after Grant's "gayness" was openly discussed. Not long ago, Dyan Cannon, Grant's fourth wife and mother of his only child, vehemently denied the rumor. But in the 1930s, it was supported by direct testimony from such friends as director George Cukor, George Burns, and Grant's later secretary, Frank Horn. Jimmy Fiedler, a powerful radio gossip columnist of the time, once sniped of Grant's very public friendship with actor Randolph Scott: "These guys are carrying the buddy business a bit too far." And actress Carole Lombard was quoted in the *Los Angeles Times* as saying: "I wonder which of those guys pays the bills." In 1980, Chevy Chase referred to him on Tom Snyder's *Tomorrow* show as a "homo." Grant sued and the case was apparently settled out of court. The last word on the subject was probably uttered by Grant himself, albeit indirectly: "I pretended to be somebody I wanted to be," he said. "And finally I became that person."

Soon after Grant and Scott met on the set of Paramount's *Hot Saturday,* also in 1932, they set up house on West Live Oak Drive near Griffith Park. Two years later, Grant carried Virginia Cherrill over the threshold of this house when, responding to pressure from Paramount, he married the actress who played the blind flower girl opposite Charlie Chaplin in *City Lights.* Standing on the doorstep to meet the newlyweds was Scott (as well as Grant's dog, Archie Leach). Eventually, however, the couple moved to the La Ronda Apartments in Hollywood, reportedly because Cherrill couldn't put up with Scott's constant presence. Scott, responding to similar studio pressure, married heiress Marian du Pont Somerville in 1936 and followed Grant to the La Ronda, where they lived in adjoining apartments.

Early in his relationship with Cherrill, Grant is said to have become so unhappy that he began drinking heavily, became surly in private, and attempted suicide at least once. The couple separated in 1935, but his drinking reportedly continued through his four subsequent marriages to heiress Barbara Hutton, actresses Betsy Drake and Dyan Cannon, and Barbara Harris, to whom he was married when he died in 1986. Scott apparently never bothered living with Somerville, sharing a life with Grant on and off for eleven years.

The pair's first home is a delightful, understated exercise in Spanish Colonial Revival architecture. It was built in 1929 for David W. Pontius, president of the Pacific Electric Company, whose famous Red Cars once scooted commuters all over the Los Angeles basin. Little is known of owners and tenants who occupied the house from the time that Grant and Scott left in the mid-1930s until it was bought in 1994 by Charles Breen, a film production designer, and his wife, Monique. "We didn't know it was Cary Grant and Randolph Scott's house when we bought it," Monique says, "a neighbor told us." What the couple did know was that the five-bedroom, 5,000-square-foot house was in terrible shape. Many tiles throughout the house had been painted over, including the Malibu tiling in the front hall. The tile roof had also been painted white and leaked in a dozen or so places. "The pool [installed in the 1960s] had three feet of green slime in it," Monique recalls, "and the living room floor was so filthy your stocking feet would stick to it." A terraced hillside had been lost for years in ivy and weeds that were eight feet deep. So the Breens launched what would become a seven-year effort to return the home to its former glory, guided

Opposite: The elegant living room and adjoining dining room. The chandelier is original, and the small door below the stairs hides a cedar-lined cabinet for storing board games.

During restoration, the owner scraped off the paint covering the original tiles with razors so as not to harm the original glaze.

Cary Grant and Randolph Scott
at home in the early 1930s.

always by their conviction that nothing should be changed that would compromise the architectural integrity of the house.

That is why, instead of removing the wall between the kitchen and the small breakfast room to create an open space more in tune with today's lifestyle, the couple renovated both rooms so that they would appear as they would have looked when cooking was done in one room and eating in another. New kitchen appliances were installed, but instead of replacing the rotted wood cabinets with modern units, the Breens had what was left of the originals painstakingly duplicated and reinstalled. Monique also spent a year removing the paint that covered tiles everywhere in the house. Fearing that paint remover would dull the finish of the original tiles, she laboriously scraped the paint off with razors; especially challenging was the downstairs bathroom where the original purple and green tiles had been covered with six coats of white, red, black, and gold paint.

The challenges seemed endless. All the floors had to be sanded, stained, and refinished, revealing beautiful inlay work. The downstairs bar room, converted in the 1960s from the home's original garage, was opened up by replacing windows and a small door with large French doors. And the broken, painted roof tiles were replaced with new handmade Spanish tiles. Along the way, the couple encountered many surprises too, among them fascinating hints of how Grant and Scott seemed to effortlessly retain their awesome physical shape. In Grant's pink-and-blue tile bathroom, mountings for an old-fashioned vibrating belt reducing machine were discovered, as well as an electric steam cabinet; the Breens converted the cabinet into a storage unit.

Opposite: The restored dining
room of the house.

Some of the house's original furnishings survived the decades of neglect, among them several stained glass windows (though others had been replaced with jalousie windows and stained glass approximations of the originals). The original living room wall sconces were still in place as was the Art Deco bronze-and-gold-colored glass chandelier in the living room (for which the Breens turned down a $30,000 offer). Underneath the stairs is a small cabinet which the present owners call a "game closet"; it is still fitted with the original cedar slots in which board games, so popular in the era, fit perfectly.

Most of the house remains as finished as when the Breens sold it in 2000. The downstairs bar/family room, however, has been converted into a music room by the new owners, and Grant's main-floor bedroom—which the Breens used as a study—has been turned into a sort of game room dominated by a large pool table (and Mr. Pontius's huge safe). The two upstairs bedrooms and their two Malibu tile lined bathrooms since have been converted into a huge master bedroom and bath. Nevertheless, a visit to the house conveys a sense of the Hollywood lifestyle of an actor on his way to the pinnacle of film fame.

Above: Downtown Los Angeles, as viewed through another of the house's unusual stained-glass windows.

This Deco delight was once Cary Grant's bathroom.

Opposite: Several smaller rooms were combined after the 1990s restoration to create the new master bedroom.

Lajeski Residence

From the birth of the film industry until the beginning of sound films in the late 1920s, the place to live was an enclave in Hollywood known as Whitley Heights. Architecturally and historically significant, today its 164 houses constitute the Whitley Heights Historic District of the National Register of Historic Places.

It was started in 1901 as a real estate development on a steep eucalyptus-and-pine-covered hill by a Canadian banker and entrepreneur named Hobart Johnstone Whitley, who, before moving to California in 1893, had founded several frontier towns in Oklahoma (including Oklahoma City). In Los Angeles he also built the railroad that linked downtown to the San Fernando Valley, where he founded a string of towns that could be served by the railroad. These towns included Van Nuys, Studio City, Sherman Oaks, and Canoga Park.

In 1903 Whitley built a Mission-style pavilion atop the western crest of his Hollywood hill to impress prospective buyers, but not much happened for fifteen years. After World War I, he turned the

Opposite: A Streamline
Moderne jewel set amid
the Spanish Colonial Revival
homes of Hollywood's
Whitley Heights enclave.
It was restored in 1986–87.

73

Aerial and hillside views of
Whitley Heights, when it was
Hollywood's best address
during the silent film era.

hill into a Mediterranean-style hill town. Buyers were given a discount if they built quickly and in the chosen style. Consequently, local architects turned out houses that introduced a look that would define the Southern California lifestyle. The style, still popular, is marked by arched doorways, red-tile roofs, huge picture windows, over-scaled terra-cotta or concrete mantles, ornate wrought iron gates and window grilles, sconces, and stippled interior walls.

Whitley Heights was an instant success. Many of Hollywood's biggest stars immediately built or moved into houses on the hill's four levels, which were linked by six stairs (some still in use). On the steepest slopes, heavy posts connected by sturdy chains were positioned to keep cars from rolling down the hill. And, very unusual for those times, all the utility wires were buried underground.

By the early 1920s, tour buses were chugging up the hill to show tourists where film greats like Francis X. Bushman (who is best remembered for his performance as Messala in the original *Ben-Hur*), Richard Barthlemess, and Rudolph Valentino lived. Valentino could often be spotted, clad in riding togs, walking his two mastiffs and his Doberman along the narrow roads. Even after stars started settling in Beverly Hills, Whitley Heights remained popular. Bette Davis lived there for a time, as did Gloria Swanson (see pp. 113–19), Greta Garbo, Maurice Chevalier, Rosalind Russell, Carmen Miranda, Leo G. Carroll, and William Powell and Carole Lombard, during their brief marriage in the early 1930s. Tyrone Power and Hermione Gingold lived

at separate times in Bushman's fabled mansion, which the actor had named Topside, though it burned down in the 1960s.

In her autobiography, Marie Dressler, one of the silent era's most famous character actors, recalled of her Whitley Heights home: "From my second-story veranda, I could see acre after acre of green California grass and bright-hues California flowers. I could watch whole regiments of royal palms march down white avenues. I lived on my little porch." Dressler loved Whitley Heights so much that she bought a second house and added a swimming pool. In 1950, about a third of the original houses were destroyed by wrecking ball and bulldozer for widening the Hollywood Freeway; among them was the house where Valentino lived longest.

Among those 164 houses in the Whitley Heights Historic District, there are a few that were not built in the community's Mediterranean style. One of these was Hobart Whitley's own place. It is built as a Palladian-style villa (it appears in the film *The Day of the Locust*). Another is the Venetian palazzo built by Eleanor De Witt in 1929 (see pp. 138–45). And in 1936, a house was built at the very top of Whitley Heights in the very latest Streamline Moderne style.

Glen Lajeski, a music business veteran and head of music creative/marketing at Disney, bought the house in 1985. Having moved from the East Coast, Lajeski thought that he should live in a tile-roof Spanish-style home. Nevertheless, within a day of seeing the place, he purchased it. "The house did it for me," he recalls. Small by Hollywood standards, the two-bedroom house measured only 3,000 square feet and,

Opposite: The second-floor stair landing's glowing warm-mustard walls express the owner's fondness for the more vibrant natural colors found locally.

The kitchen is a near-perfect restoration of the original

The master bedroom (top) and the acqua-colored sitting room, which is off the home's front hall and overlooks a pocket-sized pool.

Opposite: The living and dining rooms of the Lajeski home boast a stunning view of Los Angeles.

The guest bath still boasts its original mirrored wall etched with a Deco-style marine design.

equally uncharacteristically for Hollywood, it had no yard since it was perched on a hill. A wall was added in the 1950s along with a square swimming pool in the front courtyard.

Much of the restoration was cosmetic. In the yellow-tile kitchen, the owner replaced a window with a French door, taking care that the panes perfectly replicated window panes elsewhere in the house. The 1930s stove was kept. Surprisingly, the mirrored wall in the living room was in perfect condition as was the black glass facade of the fireplace wall. The oak floors downstairs were refinished, and, upstairs, when the indoor-outdoor carpet that covered the hall floor was ripped off, Lajeski found and restored the original Magnalite flooring (Magnalite is a poured flooring designed to look like stone). Throughout the house, the owner restored the lighting, and converted what had been a maid's apartment on the lower level into a guest suite. Both the downstairs bath, with its yellow tile and mirror etched with a fanciful marine scene, and the dramatic yellow-and-black master bathroom were in near perfect condition and needed only sprucing up.

Although Lajeski sought and received advice from a number of interior decorator friends, the final restoration decisions were his. "I didn't go by anything," he says of the result. But hidden memories had played a role; having painted the upstairs hall a warm mustard shade, he realized it was exactly the same color as his bedroom when he was young. Convenience was the first attraction of Whitley Heights. With time came its character and charm. All three qualities are embodied in this house.

Opposite: Deco at its most dramatic—the master bath.

Laughton Residence

Opposite: Nearly destroyed in an earthquake in 1994, and abandoned by a previous owner, this house, where Charles Laughton and Elsa Lanchester lived in the 1940s, was restored to its original grandeur in 2000.

The legendary actor Charles Laughton and actress wife Elsa Lanchester.

Los Angeles, like many cities, loves to destroy its cultural monuments. The Brown Derby was, for a generation, one of the most celebrated gathering places for Hollywood film stars. Today, its hat-shaped roof—a symbol once famous everywhere—has been painted puce, and sits atop a Chinese restaurant in a grimy mini mall. The fabled Cocoanut Grove nightclub as well as the hotel which sheltered it has decayed for years and is now scheduled to be torn down.

Sometimes, however, memorable homes and buildings simply slip through the cracks—they're still there, but seemingly nobody remembers. Time and fame have passed them by.

Such is the case with a house in Los Angeles's Pacific Palisades suburb which was, for nearly a decade, home to one of Hollywood's most famous actors and his similarly celebrated wife: Charles Laughton and Elsa Lanchester. In its time it was known also as the site of Laughton's private acting classes—Robert Ryan, Shelly Winters, and her roommate were among his students. The roommate's name?

The renovated kitchen, where meals were once prepared for Charles Chaplin, Paulette Goddard, and Peter Ustinov.

Marilyn Monroe. Laughton would later cast Winters in the only movie he ever directed, 1955's film noir classic, *Night of the Hunter*.

The Laughton home was celebrated for another reason among the more literary residents of Los Angeles, many of them exiles from Hitler's Germany. Over a two-year period, Laughton (who spoke no German) and the German playwright and poet Berthold Brecht (who spoke little English) somehow cobbled together an English translation of Brecht's play *Galileo*. In July 1947, six months before the play opened in New York, Laughton starred in a legendary staging of the work at the Coronet Theater on La Cienega Boulevard near Beverly Hills.

Despite their language difficulties and cantankerous personalities, Brecht and Laughton got along famously. Laughton was a dedicated gardener, and Brecht celebrated this passion in a humorous poem called "Garden in Progress." "High above the Pacific coast below it," the poem goes, "the waves' gentle thunder and the rumble of oil tankers/lies the actor's garden./Nor did the lord of the garden take in only/his own plants and trees but also/the plants and trees of his neighbors; when told this/smiling he admitted: I steal from all sides." Laughton's flowers, plants, and trees are gone, but the home's new owner has replaced them with tropical plants, giving the place a lush ambiance entirely appropriate to its Mediterranean design.

Like many actors, Laughton liked to entertain. In her autobiography, Shelly Winters celebrates the memory of dining with the Laughtons and many of Hollywood's golden-age stars, including Charlie Chaplin with his soon-to-be-ex-wife, Paulette Goddard, and the late Peter Ustinov. Few today remember that the house was known

On this stage, now a bar in the owner's home theater, Marilyn Monroe, Shelly Winters, and Robert Ryan delivered their lines in Charles Laughton's acting classes.

for something else, too—the Laughtons' famed art collection. "All over the walls of the living room and dining room were gorgeous paintings of fat naked ladies," Winters writes. She was describing Laughton's collection of paintings by the French impressionist painter Auguste Renoir; the artist's son, film director Jean Renoir (*Grand Illusion*), was a friend of the actor and helped him collect many of his father's works.

Laughton also collected more modern art and was an early fan of pre-Columbian artifacts. Broadcaster Norman Corwin once wrote a poem about his collection: "This is a house of art/In every part/In the master's can/Cezanne;/On the kitchen wall/Maillol;/Wherever you park your ass, O/It's under a Picasso." Before the art could be hung on the wall in the living room, the Laughtons had to get rid of a massive organ (complete with bells and chimes) that the home's builder had installed; it was so large that when the couple finally sold it to a church in the San Fernando Valley, it cost $3,000 to move (some $30,000 in today's dollars).

It is thus a surprise that when the present owner, entrepreneur Harold Wrobel, bought the place in 1997 in a bank foreclosure sale for $1.3 million, he had no idea who had once owned it. All he knew was that it possessed "drop-dead gorgeous views" from its site atop a 200-foot cliff overlooking the Pacific Ocean. "It was after I bought it," Wrobel says today, "that a neighbor across the street told me who once lived here. And later, Walter Matthau, who lived a block away, told me that he visited the house as a young man when the Laughtons lived here from 1941 until 1949."

Aside from that view, all Wrobel knew was that, because of damage sustained in the 1994 earthquake, the house was basically unlivable. The chimneys had fallen

Opposite: Dining room of the restored Laughton house where, in the 1940s, a priceless collection of paintings by Renoir once hung on the walls.

Opposite: The master bedroom commands a spectacular view of the Pacific Ocean.

The master bathroom was added during the house's post-earthquake restoration and renovation.

down, there were gaping holes in the walls, and hundreds of the handmade Spanish roof tiles had been shaken off. After the quake, the previous owner simply walked away from the place (hence the later foreclosure sale), thus leaving the road clear for vandals who stole all of the home's ten toilets and fixtures, ripped the kitchen cabinets from the walls, and broke hundreds of panes of window glass. "The vandals even ripped the copper wiring from the electrical junction box," Wrobel says smiling, "but they missed all the copper drains and gutters, a legacy of the copper magnate who built the villa in 1934. Because they had been painted white, I guess they thought they were plastic," he says.

It took six months, thousands of artistic and economic restoration decisions, and close to a million dollars for Wrobel and architect/designer Linda Park to bring the 9,400-square-foot villa back to life. The chimneys were rebuilt, the windows and many roof tiles were replaced, and most of the hardwood floors were refinished. Rebuilding the shattered lath and plaster interior walls and moldings was probably the toughest challenge. Wrobel recalls: "Because there was so much damage to the walls and, especially, the cornice moldings which were very intricate, it was very difficult to restore."

The vandals also missed another of the home's unique attributes: many wrought iron, Art Nouveau balcony railings made in Paris around 1900, and installed by the previous owner.

To strengthen the fragile cliffside land on which the house sits, Wrobel has "hardscaped" the bluff by covering it with tarpaulins overlaid with bricks. Additionally,

Opposite: Before restoration, the chimney and much of the roof had collapsed, and many of the windows had been broken.

Charles Laughton and Berthold Brecht wrote an English version of Brecht's play *Galileo* on the patio.

rainwater is now diverted into the city drainage system instead of eroding the bluff. It was the bluff's susceptibility to water damage that originally caused the Laughtons to move. During the summer of 1949, when the couple were on a holiday in England, a garden hose was left running, causing a large section of the actor's beloved garden to slide down the hill onto the Pacific Coast Highway. Laughton saw it as an omen, and they soon moved to a house on Curson Street in Hollywood where the actor died in 1962.

Surviving the earthquake were many of the hidden spaces that houses of this era often boasted. Among them is a secret bar off the living room (the house was started in 1932 when Prohibition was still in force). The downstairs room where Laughton hosted his acting classes was once reached by a now-closed-off secret stair. That room has been transformed into a home theater decorated with original Laughton movie posters. The stage where Monroe and Winters and their fellow students once acted now hosts a bar, but the house's original Herring-Hall-Marvin walk-in safe is still there; today it encloses a powder room.

There is another issue that many who have restored Hollywood landmarks rarely talk about but which today is the silver lining to the costly restorations. The owner of the Laughton house spent $2.3 million buying and renovating the house. Its value has been recently estimated at $10 to $14 million.

Clearly an example of having your cake and eating it too.

LombardResidence

Opposite: Poolside at the Lombard house, an icon of Moderne architecture.

Carole Lombard, one of the most beautiful and popular stars of Hollywood's golden age.

One problem with Hollywood history is that it was written in Hollywood. Thus it's history can be about as accurate as the historical epics that have come out of Hollywood studios. Every story can be improved upon, or so the thinking goes.

As we have seen, this is often the case with houses supposed to have been the home of famous stars. Many of the stars from the silent and early talkie days rented their apartments, and the rent was paid by their accountants or business managers. So, unless they did interviews at home or threw parties that were covered by the newspapers, there is no record of when, or even if, a particular star lived in a particular location.

Take Carole Lombard. She was a star at seventeen and died at thirty-three, so she wasn't around for those autumn years when stars record their lives in memoirs or reminisce to a biographer. And because Lombard died at the peak of her worldwide fame, she became an instant subject of unverifiable stories and gossip.

Clark Gable and Carole Lombard
were married in 1939.

So it is no surprise that there are a number of houses in Hollywood purported to be Carole Lombard's home. But we can be certain of only one. After actor William Daniels was fired by M.G.M. when, in 1933, he was caught having sex with a sailor at L.A.'s downtown Y.M.C.A., Lombard made a point of hiring Daniels to decorate her house.

Another house is a possible residence of Lombard's. It's grand enough (after all, Lombard was making $35,000 a week in 1939—the equivalent of $400,000 or so today); it's glamorous enough (Lombard was the very avatar of glamour in the 1930s); and it's located in Laughlin Park, still one of the most exclusive enclaves in Hollywood and popular with stars and film-industry leaders. It was also very up-to-date, designed in the Streamline Moderne style by an architect named Lester Scherer, well-known at the time as a designer of commercial buildings and churches.

Lombard was born Jane Alice Peters in Fort Wayne, Indiana, on October 4, 1908. Eight years later, her parents divorced and her mother took her and her two older brothers to Los Angeles to start a new life. At twelve, she was discovered playing baseball in the street by director Alan Dwan, who cast her as a tomboy in *A Perfect Crime*. Nothing more happened as there were enough child stars in Hollywood at the time. Determined to get into films, she quit school at fifteen (where she had excelled in athletics), joined a theater troupe, and started seriously looking for work. In 1925, Lombard passed a screen test at Twentieth Century Fox and was cast as the lead in *Hearts and Spurs*. This was followed by three more films for the studio. After she was badly injured in an automobile accident the next year (plastic surgery was necessary to repair the scarring on her face), Fox cancelled her contract. Nevertheless, she was determined and made thirteen two-reelers for the comic genius Max Sennett before landing at Pathe and then Paramount. She made the transition to talkies smoothly and soon starred in such classics as *High Voltage* (1929), *Man of the World* (1931, with William Powell whom she married, and divorced, in 1933), and *No Man of Her Own* (1932), the only movie she made with Clark Gable, her future husband.

Opposite: Facade of the Lombard house, high atop Hollywood's exclusive Laughlin Park. It was restored in 1985–86.

The impressive entrance hall (left) is crowned by a gilded Art Deco frieze. The acoustics of the music room (right) are considered perfect.

Opposite: The stunning living room of the Lombard house is designed for entertaining.

The kitchen cabinetry was fabricated from bird's eye maple, a popular wood when the house was built.

In 1934, Lombard made *Twentieth Century*, a movie that showed her true comedic talents and, in 1936, *My Man Godfrey*, for which she received her only Oscar™ nomination. By 1939, she was one of the highest paid actors in Hollywood. She picked her own projects and married Gable, an Oscar™-winning veteran of thirty-three films and soon to become world-famous for his performance as Rhett Butler in *Gone With the Wind*. In 1941, Lombard made her last film, *To Be or Not to Be*, costarring with the great comic Jack Benny, before going home to Indiana to host a war bond rally. Returning to Los Angeles on January 16, 1942, the plane carrying her, her mother, and twenty others crashed into the side of a mountain near Las Vegas, Nevada, and all were killed. Hollywood was devastated, and a grief-stricken Gable joined the Army Air Force. Lombard was posthumously awarded the Medal of Freedom by President Franklin D. Roosevelt as the first woman killed in the line of duty in World War II.

In 1985, developer Lyle Low and his wife, Rosemary, a realtor, bought a spectacular 7,300-square-foot house on a half-acre lot at the very top of the wall-enclosed, gated hill that is Hollywood's Laughlin Park. Unusual among the Spanish Colonial Revival– and Anglo Colonial Revival–style houses in the enclave, it was, from foundation to chimney, an unabashed exercise in the Streamline Moderne. The previous owner attributed the house's ownership to Lombard based on published stories to that effect. In the 1939 film, *Made For Each Other*, Carol Lombard wisecracked: "Never let the seeds stop you from enjoying the watermelon." So, despite seeds of doubt, let's enjoy the assumption that this was Lombard's home.

Designed in 1927, the house boasts many rare amenities. Each of the five bedrooms has its own bathroom. In fact, there are eight bathrooms, and each is a knockout, attributed to the fact that the builder of the house was said to have owned the largest plumbing supply company in Los Angeles. Outstanding among them are the pair of "His and Her" powder rooms that flank the front door. One is finished in lavender, green, and black tile, the other is a celebration of canary yellow and black.

Opposite: Dining in style in 1936, breathtakingly reinterpreted when the Lombard house was restored.

The most striking features are the twin ceramic lavatories in the powder room—both shaped like large tulips. The master bath, with its high ceiling and two-tone green tile, is a sybaritic delight.

The detail in the design is amazing. For example, by opening a trapdoor in the room below the garage (now a game room), it was possible to change the oil in the cars parked above. Another basement room, remodeled by an earlier owner, is now a video room, and brings the living space of the house up to 10,000 square feet. The home's music room is acoustically perfect and is crowned by a triple-cove ceiling, as are the other main-floor rooms, including the kitchen. Among the renovations made by the Lows is the kitchen. It replaced one installed in the 1950s, but the couple were careful to keep the spirit of the home by installing cabinets made from birds-eye maple, a popular wood in the 1930s. The spectacularly theatrical entrance hall, with its sweeping stair and gilded Deco frieze, is another triumph of detail. As big as most people's living rooms, it would look perfectly in place in any Hollywood movie of the time.

None of the nine original 1927 gravity furnaces that heat the place have needed replacing or repairing. (Air conditioning was added by the previous owner.) The swimming pool was installed in the 1960s, and, along with modernizing it, the Lows added a deck off the family room that overlooks the pool, seamlessly integrated into the home's overall design.

In 1951, Lucille Ball claimed that the ghost of Carole Lombard visited her in a dream and said that the hesitant Ball should take the role offered to her in what became one of early television's all-time hit shows, *I Love Lucy*. Lombard's presence is as vividly felt when visiting this house. As one recent guest said: "If Carole Lombard didn't live here, she should have."

Opposite: On a clear night, from the terrace of the Low's home, you can see, well, nearly forever.

Top: Asian-themed decor was popular in the 1930s, and it still looks right in the master bedroom.

"His" and "Her" powder rooms flank the home's entrance. The matching lavatories were designed to resemble large tulips.

Sowden–Hodel Residence

Opposite: In 1926, a retired photographer commissioned Lloyd Wright, son of Frank Lloyd Wright, to design a home for unforgettable entertaining. Restored in 2000, it still is.

A small patio off the master bath was added.

Restoration often provokes controversy, particularly when houses by celebrated architects are involved. The Hollywood house designed in 1928 by Frank Lloyd Wright Jr., is a good example.

Known as Lloyd Wright, he was a sought-after talent during Hollywood's golden age, turning out such breathtaking buildings as the lyrical Wayfarers Chapel on the Palos Verdes Peninsula and the sleek, copper-trimmed house built in 1928, which became the home of Ramon Novarro and later Diane Keaton.

Two years earlier, Lloyd Wright was hired to design a house by a retired photographer and painter named John Sowden, who asked the architect for a distinctive setting for lavish entertaining. The result, which Wright called a "grand indulgence to the obvious pleasures of the owners," was a gigantic O-shaped structure that was so successful that it still stops traffic driving by its lush setting of blue agaves and bird-of-paradise plants. The place gained notoriety following the 1999 publication of *Black Dahlia Avenger*, in which author Steve Hodel

Known locally as the "Jaws" house, because of its aggressive entrance.

An entire wall of the home's original studio, now its master bedroom, opens onto the courtyard.

(who was raised in the house after the Sowdens sold it) claimed that his father, Dr. George Hodel, was the culprit in 1947's Black Dahlia murder.

The place resembles a well-preserved Mayan temple or a temple at Angkor Wat from a Hollywood film epic, owing to its use of heavily ornamented concrete blocks, which echo the decorated blocks Wright's father designed for "Hollyhock House" (1920) and the Freeman House (1924). It is also known locally as the "Jaws" house because of the gaping prow that aggressively frames the living room window. The present owner, Xorin Balbes, who paid $1.2 million for the house in 2000, has claimed that he was given his name in a vision while visiting temples in Egypt (his given name was Randy). He says that the voice in his vision also told him: "As you had temples in the past, so shall you have temples in your lifetime."

It isn't Balbes's cosmic vision that has raised eyebrows in Hollywood—after all, people have reinvented themselves in the film capital since the beginning. It is his $3-million restoration of the house, guided by his inner voice and implemented by architect Paul Ashley and interior designer Annette Easton. Some preservationists believe that Balbes, who added a pool and fountain in the courtyard and completely modernized the bathrooms and the kitchen, has been far too liberal in his changes to an architectural treasure. Among the preservationists are purists who feel adding air-conditioning to these old houses is a sacrilege. Balbes's non-historic renovation of the kitchen into a large open room probably has been the biggest source of anger. "It's nothing more than a 'Kate Mantilini' kitchen," says one critic, referring to the open kitchen of a popular Los Angeles restaurant.

Eric Wright, the architect son of Lloyd, doesn't find the kitchen remodeling nearly as irritating as the addition of the pool and the relocation of the master bedroom from a side corridor to the "stage" (originally the home's studio) behind the courtyard. For others, including guests at the parties Balbes hosts, the pool integrates beautifully with the home's dramatic ambiance. "It's a mixed bag," Eric Wright says. "But most of

Left: The open kitchen of the house, converted from three smaller rooms, including the original kitchen, is one of the most controversial changes that Balbes made.

The dining room of the house remains where it was originally situated.

Opposite: The living room and adjoining study are, along with the home's courtyard, the center for frequent entertaining.

Opposite: The new master bath, originally a bath, darkroom and guest bedroom.

Author Steve Hodel claims in his 1999 book that his father was the infamous "Black Dahlia" murderer.

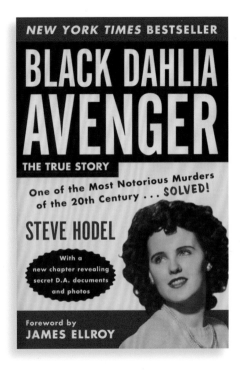

NEW YORK TIMES BESTSELLER

BLACK DAHLIA AVENGER

THE TRUE STORY

One of the Most Notorious Murders of the 20th Century . . . SOLVED!

STEVE HODEL

With a new chapter revealing secret D.A. documents and photos

Foreword by **JAMES ELLROY**

the work he did is very good." Linda Dishman of the L.A. Conservancy put her finger exactly on the challenge of restoration; people won't live in such old houses unless they are updated to provide the conveniences we take for granted today. "We need to create more of an ethic and a desire for living in these historic houses," she says. "What he [Balbes] has done makes historic houses competitive with modern ones."

Before Balbes could think about a pool or redesigning the kitchen, he had to deal with the very serious matter of keeping the place from deteriorating any more than it had. "The place was a ruin when I bought it," he says. "The first thing I had to do was to chemically stabilize the erosion of the concrete blocks . . . when you touched the walls they would turn to sand. Actually many of them had to be completely redone they were in such terrible shape. The foundation of the house also had to be rebuilt," he says. His modifications weren't easily achieved. The controversial kitchen was carved out of the original kitchen, butler's pantry, and utility room. His master bath fills the space originally occupied by a bath, a darkroom, and one of the four bedrooms in the east wing of the house.

The most challenging work encountered during the restoration was changing the entire door and window system surrounding the courtyard, replacing it with heavy sliding glass doors, which both aesthetically balanced the look of the courtyard and weatherproofed the house (there are now four heating and air-conditioning zones). "And finding the right artists to restore the ornamental concrete blocks was also a challenge," Balbes says. Because machinery couldn't get into the courtyard, the 25-x-12-foot pool (occasionally covered over to serve as a dance floor for parties) had to be dug by hand. "That was another expensive challenge," he says. But, at least for Balbes, it all turned out well. "The biggest surprise I've had is that this is the first place I've lived in that I have never tired of. Perhaps it's because its like a theater . . . throughout the day and night the environment is constantly changing."

SwansonResidence

Opposite: Gloria Swanson
lived here (twice), and William
Faulkner. It's probably another
Hollywood myth that Rudolph
Valentino also lived here, but he
did leave a souvenir.

Gloria Swanson in 1955,
five years after she starred as
Norma Desmond in *Sunset
Boulevard*.

Reality and illusion can become confused in Hollywood. And there
is no greater example than director Billy Wilder's famous 1950 noir
masterpiece *Sunset Boulevard*. For those who haven't yet seen the
film, it's the story of an ageing, once-great film star, Norma Desmond,
who lives in the past and a young journalist with whom she falls in
love. To play the role of the faded film star, Wilder first approached
Mae West, who was outraged that she was considered for the role
of a has-been actor seeking a comeback. He then asked Pola Negri
and Mary Pickford, both of whom were equally horrified. Then he
offered it to Gloria Swanson who, a generation earlier, had been
the highest-paid actress in the world. Ironically, the story of a fictional
comeback attempt would be her vehicle for a real comeback.

But the line between fact and fiction doesn't stop there. Throughout Desmond's house in the film are many framed photographs meant
to be images from the fictional star's past; in fact, they are all real
pictures of Swanson from *her* past. In the movie, Desmond screens

part of a silent film for the young reporter (played by William Holden); the film clip is actually from Swanson's 1928 movie *Queen Kelly,* made when she was being paid $250,000 a week (the equivalent of some $3 million today). And playing the role of Desmond's butler was the great director Eric von Stroheim who directed *Queen Kelly.*

Although Swanson started making movies in 1915 (when she was sixteen), her fame was really launched in 1919 when Cecil B. DeMille cast her in a number of films. In one of them, *Male and Female,* she had to enter a real lion's den and lie down with the animal. Swanson was terrified, but did it; DeMille later said she was braver than any man he had ever met. He nicknamed her "young fella," and called her that for the rest of her career. Thirty-one years later, Wilder cast DeMille in *Sunset Boulevard* playing himself directing Desmond's mock comeback where Swanson uttered the film's most famous line: "I'm ready for my close-up now, Mr. DeMille."

What is real, however, is the 3,000-square-foot house in Hollywood's Whitley Heights, which Swanson rented twice, once reportedly during the 1940s, and later when she returned to Hollywood from her home in New York to make *Sunset Boulevard.* She was so determined to live in the house that, according to the woman who owned the house for seventy years (a Mrs. Frances Whitfield), she rented it for five years. During his last stay in Hollywood in the mid-1950s, the famous author William Faulkner also rented the house for several years. Although Faulkner intensely disliked Hollywood, he apparently loved the house and would write for hours on the balcony outside the master bedroom—then used as his office. And, according to Whitfield, the first tenant of the house was none other than Rudolph Valentino, who claimed he was between houses at the time. This seems unlikely. If the place was

built in 1924 as originally believed by the present owner, Whitfield's point might be true. (There is no building record to substantiate it.) By 1925 Valentino was living in his famous Falcon Crest, and he died in New York in August 1926, at the age of thirty-one. There is some agreement that Valentino provided the plaque bearing the image of an angel on the small fountain in the entrance courtyard, yet no one has ever been able to decipher the inscription. It is possible that it was a housewarming gift. Valentino is also said to have left two upstairs chandeliers, and Swanson left the crystal chandelier in the dining room; under the home's historic site designation, those items and several others—including the garden plaque—must remain with the house.

In 2002, interior designer Martyn Lawrence-Bullard bought the place and began a complete restoration of the house. The house is shaped strangely; it bends around the corner of a small intersection, which is attributed to its being designed to fit into an oddly shaped space. Originally commissioned by Hobart Whitley, the developer of Whitley Heights, the house's designer was architect Harry McAfee.

The place needed a tremendous amount of work. Some of the present flooring is original but much of it was rotted, replaced by reclaimed wood from a barn in Idaho. Central air-conditioning and heating was installed using the original heating ducts; nevertheless, some of the original plaster was destroyed in the effort. It became necessary to locate an artisan experienced with historic plaster to make the repairs properly. The owner also wanted to open the long street wall with a window, which was not allowed under the home's historic designation.

As the garden was in terrible shape, Lawrence-Bullard had every tree and plant replaced. In the course of this work, he discovered the courtyard fountain that had

Rudolph Valentino sets out for a walk in 1923 from his long-gone "Villa Valentino" in Whitley heights with one of his mastiffs. The car is a French Voisin bearing his trademark cobra hood ornament.

Opposite: The kitchen's nineteenth-century Spanish tile floor was revealed during the restoration.

The master bathroom with its higher than normal sink, installed by Swanson so she wouldn't have to bend her bad back.

been hidden under years of undergrowth, bought the huge antique Italian oil jar that is now the centerpiece, and reopened the fountain. The kitchen floor had been covered with saltillo tiles sometime in the past, and when ripped out revealed late nineteenth-century Spanish tiles, probably imported when the house was built. In the living room, Faulkner had installed bookcases across the wall opening to the dining room, which were also removed.

The bathroom upstairs remains the way it was when modified by Swanson. She was very short (under five feet), but as she had back problems and didn't want to bend, she had the lavatory installed higher than normal. If the lavatory wasn't a problem, the rest of the bathroom certainly was. It needed replumbing and so, as not to destroy the original tile work, Lawrence-Bullard went to the extraordinarily expensive option of replacing the plumbing from the outside. "What we didn't know was that the floor was completely rotted. The day before I moved in," Lawrence-Bullard laughs, "the bathtub and the tile around it came straight down through the living room ceiling." As the tub had not broken anything when it fell (it missed a rare chest in the living room by only inches), they were able to build a scaffold around the tub, raise it straight up, and rebuild the floor under it. Near the spot where the tub came through the ceiling, the original mantle had been removed—the owner replaced it with one of Italian marble.

"The house reminded me of a place in Southern Italy or in Spain," Lawrence-Bullard explains, "so I decided to go with traditional Spanish colors of red, black, and white, and stain the floors dark." Then he furnished the house mostly with

Opposite: Owner Lawrence-Bullard's guest room was once Gloria Swanson's maid's room and the place where she stored her hundreds of pairs of shoes.

Opposite: This deck off the
master bedroom was William
Faulkner's favorite place to
write during his last stay in
Hollywood in the 1950s.

Rudolph Valentino gave the
small plaque bearing the image
of an angel installed below
the fountain in the entrance
courtyard.

eighteenth-century Italian and Portuguese furniture with Moorish touches. He deviated from this when furnishing the dining room. Under Gloria Swanson's chandelier, the dining table is surrounded by chairs made for the marriage of a Portuguese princess to a Russian prince in 1720, but the showstopper in the room is a sixteenth-century inlaid-ebony breakfront from Lawrence-Bullard's family.

Upstairs, the room which William Faulkner used as his office is once again the master bedroom. Today, according to the owner's plan, it is furnished with an eighteenth-century Portuguese bed, and among the valuable paintings in the room is one from 1670 by Andrea Sarti of a naked slave. In the course of restoring this room, the original painted hearth of the tiny fireplace was revealed. Nearby is a little bedroom that, when Swanson was there, functioned as both a maid's room and a shoe room, filled with the actress's shoe collection (her feet were so small that when she found a pair that fit, she tended to buy them by the dozen). Next to this room is the door to the biggest surprise in the house. "Unlike most of the houses in here," Lawrence-Bullard says, "many of these houses were built for film stars. So all of them had big closets which you find hardly anywhere else in houses built at that time in Hollywood."

TalmadgeBeachHouse

Opposite: Silent screen star Norma Talmadge's beach house in Santa Monica. It was restored by the present owners in the early 1980s.

Norma Talmadge (right) and her sister Constance, ca. 1923.

In February 1931, *Motion Picture Classic* ran a story titled "The End of the Road," a moody piece by Gladys Hill based on an interview with the world-famous screen star Norma Talmadge at her beach house. "We sat by a wide long window facing a gray sea, in Norma's house on Santa Monica Beach," Hill wrote. "The sky was as gray as the water. Gulls winged and wheeled and cried, mournfully. A pastel of the young Norma hung on one wall, smiling confidently. A portrait, silver framed, of Joseph Schenck dominated one corner. A little old organ, a hundred years old, brought from France, stood against a wall. It brought a thought of the more gentle, ivoried fingers that had played it and now play no more. There was a sense of passing things."

"Passing things" was a reference to Talmadge's career; like many silent film stars, Norma Talmadge was unable to make the transition from silent films (where she started with the Vitagraph Company at the age of fourteen) to talkies. *DuBarry, Woman of Paris*, a talkie

The patio of the Talmadge
beach house.

In 1929, even beach houses could be formal. The entrance hall of the Talmadge house in Santa Monica.

she made in 1930 for United Artists, had recently been released and the reviews were devastating. "Norma Talmadge, who has been the very heart of the heart of movies, *means* motion pictures to most of us over twenty or twenty-five," Hill added. "If Norma's link with the movies breaks, something will be severed, something will be gone that not all the Garbos and the Dietrichs in the world can ever replace." In his 1934 novel, *Tender is the Night*, F. Scott Fitzgerald enshrined her as the epitome of 1920s glamour, as one who "must be a fine, noble woman beyond her loveliness."

Not only was Talmadge's link with the movies ending, so too was her marriage to Joseph Schenck, whom she married in 1917 and who supervised the majority of her films. The couple separated in 1930 (the same year as *DuBarry*) and divorced in 1934. Talmadge then married actor and comic George Jessel (nicknamed America's "Toastmaster General" for his countless appearances at political and corporate events), and, after divorcing him in 1939, she married Dr. Carvel James.

Built for Talmadge in 1929 on the shifting sands of Santa Monica Bay, the house in which the interview was conducted was built on a surer foundation than Hollywood fame. The house was designed in a style which might be described as Hollywood-Tudor-by-the-sea by set designer and architect Paul R. Crawley and no expense was spared in its construction. The actress wanted a prime location and she paid $2,000 a foot for the sixty-foot lot. She spent $450,000 on the house, a stunning figure at the time—particularly as the Great Depression hit only months after the house was completed.

Aside from its oceanside location, another attraction of the site was the presence of many film-industry neighbors who owned beach houses nearby; among them were Marion Davies, Louis B. Mayer, Irving Thalberg (M.G.M.'s brilliant production director) and his wife, Norma Shearer, and Norma's sister, Constance, also a successful actress, who lived next door in a house also designed by Crawley. Norma also

Opposite: The spacious living room, whose celebrity tenants once included Howard Hughes and British actor Brian Aherne.

The dining room of the Talmadge house was redecorated by Barbara Hutton in 1942 to resemble her favorite Paris restaurant, Maxim's.

bought the lot just south of her house; she later sold it to actor Leo McCarey who gave it to the City of Santa Monica, which tore it down and today uses the site as a beach parking lot.

Part of the high cost of the house was to insure that it would be as secure as if it were located in downtown Hollywood, even when it was exposed to ocean storms. Huge creosoted pilings were driven deep into the sand, to which heavy timbers were bolted and cross braced. Everything—house, gardens, and swimming pool—was constructed on this foundation.

After marrying Dr. Carvel James and moving to the East Coast, Talmadge sold the house to Cary Grant, who lived there with Randolph Scott. There is a story that Grant and Scott loved the place so much that they agreed that whichever of them remarried first would have the right to own it. It didn't quite work out that way. Within a month after becoming an American citizen, on June 26, 1942, Grant married the Woolworth heiress Barbara Hutton. But Scott stayed. Hutton once recalled of the *ménage à trois*: "That fellow never did move out. He was always in a back room somewhere."

Grant installed a luxurious dressing room for himself; it's still there, little changed from the days when the elegant cherry-wood chest was filled with his custom-made shirts. Hutton tried to turn the place into a sort of Paris-West. As World War II raged, she declared: "If I can't go to Paris, Paris must come to me." This meant redesigning a bar in the sunroom and adding carved woodwork in the downstairs powder room (the carved mirror, towel bar, toilet-roll holder, and toilet seat are still there). It also meant transforming the dining room into a space reminiscent of her favorite Paris restaurant, Maxim's. Deep ruby-red plush banquettes seating twenty-four at silver-colored tables were installed around the room, whose slate floor was covered with matching red carpet. On the walls, gold-flecked, smoked-glass mirrors were installed.

During restoration, owner Jennifer Diener spent two weeks removing pink nail polish previously painted on the Egyptian themed Art Deco tiles of the master bathroom.

Opposite: Barbara Hutton probably never prepared a meal in the now-beautifully modernized kitchen.

Grant filled the pool with fresh water rather than sea water, which was the custom at beach houses of the time. "After all," he remarked, "if I want to bathe in sea water all I have to do is open the gate, go down the steps and walk in." He added a filter but neglected a heater.

By 1945 the marriage was on its last legs. Hutton was always difficult, and Grant thought she had a tendency to mistake a film star's screen persona for his or her real self. "She thought she was marrying Cary Grant," he said. Not long before their divorce the couple moved to a larger house, and Scott, who married Patricia Stillman in 1944, took over the house (they would have two children and remain married for forty-three years until the actor's death in 1987).

In 1946 Scott sold the house to British actor Brian Aherne and his new wife, who kept it until the present owners, Royce and Jennifer Diener, bought it in 1979. Occasionally the Ahernes rented the place; most notably to Howard Hughes (who topped the walls with barbed wire—some of it remains).

Aherne, who made few changes other than adding a volleyball court, claimed that Grant always regretted selling it to Scott, often asking Aherne in later years, "Oh, sell it back to me." Aherne claims that Grant added: "Come to think of it, I don't think Randy ever paid me for the place."

One of the first things the new owners did was to rip out the banquettes. In the process they discovered the frames for a pair of French doors opening from the dining room into the sun room, and were able to replicate the doors themselves from the original blueprints. The couple also discovered in the home's trunk room—now the wine cellar—the original Italianate sconces that were replaced by Hutton's fake Towle lamps. The dining room's smoked-glass mirrors were removed except for one

Cary Grant had this shirt cabinet built in what is now Royce Diener's dressing room, which is adjacent to the master bedroom.

wall, which the Dieners kept as an "homage to Barbara Hutton." Little else has been changed aside from adding security grilles, and bricking over the cheap-looking cement coping surrounding the pool, and modernizing the kitchen as well as enlarging it by eliminating a pantry. In Hutton's bathroom they replaced a pink carpet with tile appropriate to its Egyptian-themed, Art Deco design (Jennifer Diener spent two weeks and a quart or so of nail polish remover stripping pink polish from the orange lotus leaves on the bathroom tiles). The 1994 earthquake hit Santa Monica particularly hard, and severely damaged the flat red tiles (handmade in Arkansas according to Aherne) on the steeply pitched roof. Enough were rescued to retile the highway side with originals, and close matches were used to recover the roof on the ocean side.

The house still stands today, comfortably ensconced by its walls alongside the Pacific Coast Highway where thousands of cars zip by every day. Few drivers suspect that they are speeding past one of the most glamorous residences of Hollywood's golden age.

Opposite: The upstairs study of the house commands a postcard view of the beach and ocean.

"**Talmadge**Residence"

Opposite: Built in 1926, in Hollywood's Los Feliz neighborhood, the Cedars was inspired by a Spanish palace. It was restored in 2002.

A ruby glass window in a guest bathroom.

In 2004, a record was set in Los Feliz, a hip neighborhood adjoining Hollywood, when a restored 1926, six-bedroom, 13,000-square-foot mansion perched atop a steep half-acre knoll was sold to a clothing designer for $5.3 million. It's certain that the controversy surrounding both the earlier $2.5 million, fourteen-month restoration of the house as well as the identity of the original tenant will persist.

This house, now called The Cedars, has long been known as the "Talmadge House," but there is no proof that the legendary silent screen actress Norma Talmadge ever set foot in the place. She did, apparently, live at one time in the area, and a nearby street is called Talmadge Avenue. (See pp. 120–29 for a house that she did live in). Norma had two sisters who also were in film: Constance, most famous as the Babylonian mountain girl in D.W. Griffith's *Intolerance* (1916), and Natalie, who made several pictures with Buster Keaton before marrying him in 1921 and retiring into happy motherhood.

Ceiling detail in the Cedars.

The sales material for the house claimed it had been "reputedly" the home of Talmadge (as well as the late Jimi Hendrix and Rod McKuen). No such restraint was exercised by the *Los Angeles Times* or by the seller who asserted on television that The Cedars was indeed the home of Norma Talmadge and her husband, Joseph Schenck. The couple might have shared it for a time, but it is highly unlikely that Schenck, then head of United Artists Studio and soon-to-be president of Twentieth Century Fox, would hardly have been comfortable in a house festooned with replicas of Leo the Lion, symbol of the rival studio, M.G.M.

The house, a mixture of styles—no architect was named in the original, 1926 sales material—was billed as a replica of the Duke of Alba's palace in Spain. Built for a Philip Hunt, and perhaps designed by S. Charles Lee (city building records indicate that Lee designed the property's garage/servants' quarters building), it was sold in 1969 to a U.C.L.A. professor who used it as a private book repository, and occasionally rented out rooms.

Much of what the recent seller did is acceptable in updating an old house to meet today's lifestyle. The swimming pool added in the back yard is gorgeous, the modern kitchen is a cook's delight, and the aggressive modernization of the bathrooms, somewhat startling in the context of the rest of the house, is, however, interesting. In addition, the roof over the entire western end of the house, boasting tremendous views, was completely reengineered to serve as a spectacular site for entertaining guests. The restorer also added a gym and a wine cellar on the lower level of the house and built a curved courtyard entrance in the front of the house, which originally opened directly onto the street.

Opposite: The huge ballroom/ living room and, on the left, the adjoining solarium of the Cedars. The M.G.M. lions on the mantels and the bas-reliefs between the beams were a later addition.

An opulent bathroom in the Cedars (detail of the ruby glass window appears on page 131).

Opposite: The master bedroom could easily serve as a set for a 1920s film.

One of the biggest challenges was "creating a yard space for the house where there wasn't any," the restorer says. "There was really no property so I built foundation walls and backfilled to create courtyards." Another problem was that the house, like many of the era, was very dark. So he put in windows (thirty percent of the windows are new). This was done so unobtrusively that an expert would have a tough time telling the original fenestrations from the new ones. "Also, a big problem was dealing with a building that was made of hollow clay blocks," he says. "Remodeling that sort of construction is far different than remodeling or restoring one of stucco and framing. Many of the commercial buildings in Los Angeles were built of hollow clay blocks in the 1920s; they were larger and lighter than brick. But when you go into them to add new windows or doors, then you have to frame the openings with steel and concrete. It was a big job." His happiest surprise in the restoration? "Everyone loves the scale of the ballroom. But I think my greatest surprise is how well the rooms flow together."

Everyone also loves the enormous ballroom (46 × 23 × 32 feet) and the adjacent solarium/music room (equally large at 42 × 22 feet). But why are all those gold-painted replicas of M.G.M.'s celebrated symbol, Leo the Lion, crouching on the mantels, and why are all those bas-reliefs of Leo's face glaring down from high up on the living room walls?

The doubts begin the moment one walks into the house's 28-foot-high entrance foyer with its "Rococo dome fresco ceiling" (*Los Angeles Times*). Look closely at those "frescoes." They may have been frescoes once but the images on the ceiling of the foyer now seem to have been clipped out of art books and magazines and glued up there sometime in the past. Among them are reproductions of paintings by

Goya, Gainsborough, Michelangelo, Leonardo da Vinci (the *Mona Lisa*), and even a "Sacred Heart of Jesus" image familiar from countless religious calendars. And what are those baroque-looking designs in the coffers of the dining room ceiling made from? Crumpled paper painted gold? That's what it looks like. And are the distressed floors original? (No.)

But many see it all as glamorous. On a warm night with all the doors open to ocean breezes, the sound of seven fountains, and filled with an "A-list" crowd, it certainly conveys that impression.

Maybe that's because this is, after all, Hollywood. "How do I feel about people saying that the house is over the top?" the restorer asks rhetorically. "You have to have a sense of humor. You go through the door and see all that decoupage on the ceiling and realize that this is a joke about Hollywood. I think the house is a fine example of what Hollywood itself is . . . over the top."

"Strip away the phony tinsel of Hollywood," the late entertainer Oscar Levant quipped, "and you find the real tinsel underneath." To many The Cedars is the real tinsel.

Opposite: The swimming pool was a later addition.

The northwest facade. The entrance is in the background and one of the home's many fountains is centered in the courtyard to the left.

VillaVallombrosa

Opposite: Living room of the Villa Vallombrosa, built in 1929 by Eleanor De Witt, an antiques dealer.

M.G.M. costume designer Adrian and his future wife, Janet Gaynor (winner of the first Best Actress Oscar¹), were early residents of the house.

Like many cities, there are parts of Los Angeles where turning a corner can plunge you into another time. Such a place is Hollywood's Whitley Heights.

But unique even for Whitley Heights is a tiny intersection called Watsonia Terrace. Unlike much of Los Angeles, the setting—a sort of cul-de-sac surrounded by houses that look like they came out of an Italian opera set in a sub-tropical ambience—never fails to entrance the visitor. And, since the 1920s, the romantic theatricality of the setting has attracted scores of talented people who will do anything to live there.

The Villa Vallombrosa, in particular, has captivated creative people; so many, in fact, that a recent publication called it "the House of Oscars™" after they "discovered" that nearly everyone who lived there prior to 1949 either won or was nominated for an Oscar™. Like many Hollywood stories, this turned out to be another myth;

Left: Facade of the Villa Vallombrosa, a Venetian fantasy in the
heart of Hollywood.

Downstairs hall of the villa.
Rather than being subjected to
a major restoration, it has been
maintained throughout the years
by a series of minor renovations,
the most recent in the 1980s.

The Villa Vallombrosa, ca. 1950.

several of the residents were nominated for or won Oscars™, before or after the time they lived in the house.

Its facade would look hopelessly eccentric anywhere but in Venice—or Hollywood. In Hollywood, houses bearing Norman battlements, apartments designed like Napoleon III's Paris, Hansel and Gretel houses, and buildings copied after castles in Spain don't appear out of place at all. For many film stars, going home from a day working on a movie set of Robin Hood's Sherwood Forest to a home that resembles Anne Hathaway's cottage seems normal.

In the Preface, I recalled Mercedes de Acosta's remembrance of the movie-set feeling of the Villa Vallombrosa, confirmed when, in the early 1930s, a large boulder rolled down the hillside behind the house, crashed through the wall, and settled itself among the group of guests. Such a lack of structural integrity was not an over-riding concern of the house's builder, Eleanor DeWitt, nor of the architect, Norman Coleman, when the 3,000-square-foot house was designed in 1929. DeWitt, an antiquarian dealing in European furniture and objets, had decided she wanted something Italianate after making a number of trips to Italy. She first sent Coleman to Tuscany for inspiration, and then on to Venice, apparently because she wanted a house more evocative of the serene republic than a Medician fortress.

Given the design of certain features such as the columns and fireplace in the Villa Vallombrosa, DeWitt must have picked up some design cues from her friend Addison Mizner, the architect/developer of Boca Raton, Florida, where he introduced the Mediterranean Revival style of architecture that still defines the lifestyle of many wealthy Floridians.

The romantic courtyard in the Villa Vallombrosa where, in 1931, Greta Garbo and M.G.M costume designer Adrian planned her outfits for Mata Hari.

In April 1932, film costume designer Adrian (born Adrian Adolph Greenberg in 1903, he used only his first name professionally) rented the house from DeWitt. He was famed as M.G.M.'s top house costume designer, best remembered today as the man who not only created Joan Crawford's narrow-hipped, broad-shouldered look, but also the ruby-red slippers worn by Judy Garland in *The Wizard of Oz*.

When Adrian rented the house, he and the celebrated actress Janet Gaynor were definitely considered a couple (they wouldn't marry until 1935). Gaynor was already famous for winning the first Best Actress Oscar™ at the 1929 Academy Awards (it was given for three films she made in 1927 and 1928, among them *Seventh Heaven* and *Sunrise*). She would go on to star in the original 1937 version of *A Star Is Born*, a film for which she was again nominated for the Best Actress award, losing to Louise Rainer for her performance in *The Good Earth*. The next resident of the house was Omar Kiam, the costume designer for *A Star Is Born*. He lived in the house for a year after Adrian moved out in October 1934. The only other Academy Award won by a resident of the house was awarded to Ben Hecht, who received it in 1929 for the screenplay for *Underworld*. Hecht, who with Charles MacArthur wrote the sensationally successful 1928 play *The Front Page* (it would be made into four films, most notably *His Girl Friday*, the 1940s version with Cary Grant and Rosalind Russell), lived in the house in 1942. He and MacArthur would share another Oscar™ in 1935 for *The Scoundrel*.

Despite his professional eminence, Adrian, who designed costumes for 233 films, never won an Oscar™ because the award for costume design was added only after

Opposite: Annie Kelly and Tim Street-Porter's sitting room in their Venetian villa.

Other than the addition of modern appliances, the kitchen is little changed from 1929, when the house was built.

he retired in the late 1940s. The house was also home to photographer Baron Adolf de Meyer, from November 1936 until November 1937. Leonard Bernstein, who lived in the house during a summer in the mid-1940s, while he was conducting at the Hollywood Bowl, never won an Academy Award but was later nominated for the film score of 1954's *On the Waterfront.* Other celebrity tenants of the period include Metropolitan Opera baritone John Charles Thomas, playwrights Victor Wolfson and Nathaniel Curtis, and Dame Judith Anderson, who lived in the house from 1947 to 1949. After renting the place out for all these years, DeWitt enjoyed the house for a few years until she died in the Villa in 1961.

Despite the numerous renters, the house has remained in remarkable condition through the years. Since DeWitt's death, subsequent owners removed many anachronistic fixtures and friezes, restored the roof, moved one bathroom and updated the others, and updated the kitchen. Otherwise, this "prop" of a house weathered the generations well. "When they first built this house, some people thought it looked phony, like a stage set," Kelly says. "But time has given it character and an authenticity."

Opposite: The master bedroom.

VinmontResidence

Above and opposite: The Vinmont house, designed in 1925. In the background is Hollywood's famous Griffith Park Observatory.

Born in 1890 in Indiana, architect Roland E. Coate Sr. arrived in Los Angeles in 1919 after working with one of Manhattan's top commercial design firms and serving in France with the American Expeditionary Forces. Despite a thorough indoctrination in the baroque Beaux-Arts style then espoused at Cornell University's School of Architecture (think New York's Grand Central Station), Coate brought something unique to a community whose architecture was characterized by fussiness—a spare simplicity that even eighty years later, looks freshly minted.

Although Coate also designed English Tudor and American Colonial Revival homes, his most popular designs were based on a Mediterranean idiom that, by the 1920s, was becoming intimately woven into the psychology of the population. In partnership with the British émigré architect Gordon B. Kaufmann, Coate started designing buildings that honored but greatly simplified the traditional geometry of the Mediterranean style, thus achieving a rare elegance. This

was recognized in an October 1939 issue of *Pencil Points*, which described his designs as, "central in the development of the informal, comfortable and open style house . . . regarded by many as the finest expression of California residential work." Among Coate's well-known clients were the director Frank Capra, producer David O. Selznick, and stars such as Gary Cooper, Robert Taylor, and Barbara Stanwyck. Howard Hughes once bought a Coate house although it had not been designed for him. (Kaufmann's work would evolve in the next decade from the Mediterranean into Art Deco, expressed in such design triumphs as the *Los Angeles Times* building.)

The most familiar of Coate's contributions is Beverly Hills's All Saints' Episcopal Church, designed in 1924, which, with its unadorned facade, simplifies Mediterranean style to an extreme. Another less radical approach was the home he designed for the president of the California Petroleum Corporation, Jacques Vinmont, the next year.

Located at the edge of Hollywood's exclusive Laughlin Park enclave, the Vinmont house was recognized as a masterpiece from the day it was finished. *Pacific Coast Record* featured photographs and floor plans of the house in its March 1927, issue; two months later *The Architectural Record* did the same. Located on a one-acre lot, with the garage and pool, the 7,000-square-foot house cost $77,492.17 to build, a huge sum when most tract-type homes could be bought for a twentieth of that sum.

The Vinmonts got their money's worth: a Mediterranean-style mansion, L-shaped (allowing a sheltered garden) with a hipped tile roof. The two-story entrance hall featured a sweeping stair; a large living room measuring 22 × 30 feet (with 12-foot ceilings) was anchored on a giant, 7-foot Italian carved marble fireplace (its off-center alignment was dictated by the then-ubiquitous grand piano); and a dining room and library boasted coffered, stenciled ceilings. Off the living room was a patio and

The large kitchen was created by combining the original kitchen and several adjoining rooms.

Opposite: Architect Roland Coate's signature style was an ultra-simplified Mediterranean look, which works well with both the traditional and the modern furniture in the dining room today.

loggia, situated around a fountain and surrounded by a lovely arcade. In an homage to early filmmaking, the patio was sheltered from the sun by canvas sheets suspended on wires, in exactly the same way sunlight was earlier controlled on Hollywood's outdoor sets. There was a three-car garage, over which was a four-room apartment and, somewhat unusually for the era, a large (18 × 30 feet, with a depth of 10 feet) swimming pool.

The Vinmonts sold the house in March 1939 to a designer of theater organs, and, following his death, the house was bought by Bernard Flynn, president of the Pacific Soap Company, in 1956. He and his wife lived there for thirty-two years, during which they walled the property and enlarged the kitchen (they raised twelve children in the house). Everything else remained as it was until 1993, when new owners embarked on a complete, multimillion dollar restoration of the house, which took two and a half years.

Brian Tichenor whose Tichenor-Thorp firm did the restoration recalls that the house was "totally beat to hell. But Roland Coate was so accomplished as an architect," he adds, "all we had to do was look carefully, and we knew what to do." In addition to the expected restoration challenges (like dry rot, repairing the roof, insulating roof and walls, and replacing the plumbing and wiring), there were some surprises. Among them, he says, was the use of oddly chosen wood here and there. "The stair hall was alder which makes no sense at all (because of its light color)." The biggest change was the kitchen, today an amalgam of the original kitchen and several small rooms. A maid's room was later converted into a gym for the present owners, a film director and his wife, who bought the place in 1996.

The patio and surrounding loggia.

Opposite, top: The master
bedroom.

Opposite, bottom: Finding
or replicating period tile
and hardware for the master
bathroom as well as the other
bathrooms was a challenging
part of the restoration.

New grilles for the added air-conditioning openings were designed to be compatible with the rest of the house; so, too, the tiles and hardware chosen for the new bathrooms. "At one time," the present owners laugh, "a decorator bomb went off; some of the ceilings were painted orange, and there were murals painted on the floors." It was apparently the same decorator who was responsible for the loss of a lot of the house's original furniture. The furnishings picked by the present owners are an eclectic combination of modern and 1940s pieces. It all works well, especially impressive are the large sofas in the living room upholstered in a greenish-gray silk and set on a gray silk rug.

The conservation habits of the early twentieth century provided another surprise: the water in the patio fountain was not recirculated but just overflowed into the city sewer system. Today the fountain has been restored to working order, but it has not been reworked to conserve water and is rarely used. The couple has replaced the original canvas sheets that sheltered the patio.

The use of the bedrooms has been changed into what is now a three-bedroom, four-bath home. One bedroom was situated off the living room following the tradition of past years, when parents, who might not easily negotiate stairs, lived with their children; it has been converted into a TV room. And recently the couple just completed restoring the swimming pool, pulling off all the old tile so that earthquake cracks could be repaired, and installing a medium blue-colored glass tile, which now covers the entire interior.

There is the saying "God is in the details," says Tichenor. "And it's especially true in restoring one of these wonderful houses...their life and character lives in such details as the moldings and tile and hardware."

Scenes

ChandlerResidence

As noted in the Preface, many of the houses visited in this book are based on fantasy, designed to resemble Mayan temples, Venetian palazzi, and the like. The design of this house, however, drew its roots from the classical wellspring that inspired the designs of many turn-of-the-century palaces funded by banking and corporate tycoons along New York City's Fifth Avenue and in Newport, Rhode Island. The style is called Beaux-Arts.

Based on ideas taught at Paris's legendary École des Beaux-Arts between 1885 and 1920, this style was widely proselytized by many American graduates of the school. It is characterized by a grandiosity derived from formal planning and frequently over-rich decoration and the use of columns, pilasters, and balustrades. Accordingly, it quickly became the favorite for courthouses, museums, and railroad terminals. By the mid-twentieth century, the style had fallen from popularity. Frank Lloyd Wright called Beaux-Arts homes and buildings "Frenchite pastry."

Opposite: For years, the seat of power in Los Angeles was this 1911 Beaux-Arts mansion, home to *Los Angeles Times* publisher Norman Chandler and his dynamic wife, Dorothy Buffum ("Buff") Chandler.

The formal living room of the Chandler mansion.

Opposite: As in the entrance hall, much of the downstairs of the Chandler mansion is sheathed in intricately decorated walnut and mahogany paneling.

But in 1911, when architects J. Martyn Haenke, William Dodd, and Julia Morgan designed a house for Dr. Peter Janss here on Lorraine Boulevard in what is now the Hancock Park section of Los Angeles, Beaux-Arts was the last word in design. Morgan was born in San Francisco and studied at the École des Beaux-Arts (after being refused admission for two years because of her gender). Among her most famous designs and collaborations are the Fairmont Hotel in her home town; the iconic Hopi gift shop at the Grand Canyon; and numerous projects for publisher William Randolph Hearst, including his flamboyant San Simeon estate, the *Los Angeles Examiner* building, and Ocean House, the gigantic beach house in Santa Monica designed for Hearst and his mistress, the actress Marion Davies.

A mansion designed in the latest style was important to Dr. Janss. Janss was a major figure in the development of Los Angeles. He arrived in the city in 1893 to practice medicine, but by 1906 he had discovered there was a lot more money in property than in prescriptions, and formed an investment company with his sons Edwin and Harold. The still relatively exclusive Hancock Park enclave was one of his projects, but it was secondary to his success in subdividing L.A.'s Boyle Heights neighborhood (where buyers were lured with purchase plans as low as $5 down and $5 a month); Van Nuys and Canoga Park in the San Fernando Valley; and, on a 10,000-acre ranch, much of Thousand Oaks. But the Janss family's most significant development was elsewhere. In 1911, the same year he built his Beaux-Arts mansion, Janss bought a 3,000-acre ranch on the city's west side, on which he convinced the state to build U.C.L.A. Then, surrounding the campus, he developed Westwood, today one of the city's most popular neighborhoods.

The 9,500-square-foot house was built on a one-acre site, which also hosted a guest cottage, a three-car garage with a staff apartment, and a reflecting pool,

Above: The huge dining room is sheathed in *boiserie* from a French chateau.

The large kitchen was created from several smaller rooms, including the home's original silver safe.

Opposite: The mansion's music room, site of many fund raising events hosted by Mrs. Chandler.

and was lavishly finished. Acres of walnut and oak paneling cover the walls of the entrance hall and living room, which also boasts eighteenth-century columns and a wall fresco from a Venetian palazzo. The formal dining room is paneled in eighteenth-century *boiserie* from a French château. The spectacular kitchen and family room encompass four rooms that were combined, but many of the details—faucets, sinks, and the like—are original. The downstairs room that impresses people most is the 32-x-23-foot music room. It was brought from an Austrian or German castle—*boiserie*, hand-painted silk panels, and all. Although erroneously described as "originally created for Wolfgang Amadeus Mozart," the room probably does date from the late eighteenth century and could well have been one of the many where Mozart played during his tours as a child prodigy.

It was a spectacular setting for the fund-raising parties hosted by the wife of the next owner of the house, who had decided to save the Hollywood Bowl. She went on to use the house as a stage when she raised $19 million to build the city's Music Center complex in the early 1960s, an accomplishment honored by a December 1964 *Time* cover. She was Mrs. Norman Buffum Chandler, once universally known as "Buff."

It was during this time that the house assumed its position—unchallenged for decades—as the seat of true power in Los Angeles. The main reason for this was Buff's husband, Norman Chandler, publisher from 1944 to 1960 of the *Los Angeles Times*, who oversaw the transformation of the paper from a conservative regional journal into one of the largest and best respected papers in the country. (Buff had more than a little to do with this change in the paper; at the 1952 Republican convention, when Norman was leaning toward an endorsement of the conservative Robert

The master bedroom.

Opposite: During the restoration, many of the original fixtures including the cast iron bathtub were preserved in the master bath.

Golden age grandeur—the restored Chandler mansion by night.

Taft, Buff took him aside and told him she would never sleep with him again if he did. Norman switched his support to the more moderate Dwight Eisenhower.) In 1960, he was succeeded as publisher by the couple's son, Otis.

After the Chandlers bought the place in 1950, they named it *Los Tiempos*—"The Times" in Spanish. They moved from the Pasadena area so Buff could be nearer Jewish enclaves like the Hillcrest Country Club, a major source for arts-related fund-raising. As long as Norman lived, the powerful and the famous beat a path to his door, including presidents-to-be Nixon, Kennedy, and Johnson, all of whom stayed in the upstairs bedroom next to the publisher's small exercise room when seeking Chandler's support. After Norman's death in 1973, Buff Chandler continued to reign as the city's grandest dame until her death in 1997 at the age of ninety-six.

Not long ago, the house was bought by designers Kathleen Scheinfeld and Timothy Corrigan. They have since removed an outside wall built by the Chandlers so their guests wouldn't have to see the servants working in the kitchen wing, repainted several rooms in appropriate colors, and planted many new trees on the property.

Standing on a credenza at the top of the sweeping staircase is a marble bust of the Roman Emperor Nero. To some visitors this may be seen as an impressive part of the furnishings of the mansion, or to those of a more cynical bent, as an accurate metaphor for the absolute power exercised by the publisher and the breathtaking majesty of the house itself.

Not even the legendary opulence of Nero's fabled "Golden House" on Rome's Esquiline Hill could match what the *Los Angeles Times* recently called, "without a doubt, one of L.A.'s grandest homes."

Opposite: The study adjoining the music room.

ElCabrilloApartments

The impulse to restore an historic apartment building is different from that which prompts a house restoration. You're not restoring your own home, but places to be occupied by a turnover of tenants. Accordingly, there is less of a demand for the highest quality materials and workmanship.

This mind-set is magnified when, as in Los Angeles, booming real estate prices have recently far outstripped the ability of apartment owners to increase revenues regulated under rent control or rent stabilization. What might have been a profitable rental income when the apartment building was worth $2 million, is no longer economically viable when the property's value soars to $5 million and rents, under the city's present stabilization law, can be increased only 3 percent per year. Landlords can make life so miserable for the tenants that they move—allowing the landlord to increase the rent to the market level between tenants—or landlords can cut back on maintenance. Either way, the building suffers.

Opposite: "It's like living in a movie set," says one resident of Hollywood's El Cabrillo fountain-courtyard apartments.

Detail of the entrance of one apartment; the living room is to the left, the dining room and kitchen are in the background (right). The building was constructed of concrete blocks, specially compounded, sized, and rusticated to resemble adobe bricks.

Opposite: Restored in the early 1990s, the El Cabrillo apartments, built in 1927, were inspired by a Spanish villa.

Take the case of the El Cabrillo apartment building. It was built in 1927, probably financed by Cecil B. DeMille, to provide housing for New York stage actors who were needed when sound was coming in for their reliable voices.

The ten-unit building was designed by Arthur Zwebell, a self-educated man with a passion for automobiles and talent for invention and design (he once designed a custom roadster body for the Model T Ford). He and his wife, Nina, who designed many of his interiors, moved to Los Angeles in 1921 and began designing single-family homes. Their fame, however, would be based on the seven or eight courtyard apartments they designed, beginning with one styled as a Hansel and Gretel fantasy. The couple never had an office, but operated out of their own home, hiring architects and engineers to sign off on their plans.

It is the Zwebell's flair for fantasy that makes their courtyard apartments like the El Cabrillo so popular. Inspired by a villa in Andalusia, the El Cabrillo was constructed of concrete blocks rusticated to look like stone-colored adobe brick, unlike the Zwebells' other apartments, which were built of wood and stucco. Many of the units boasted several Zwebell signature design elements: two-story living rooms, mezzanines, and graceful staircases. Many of the stair risers and settees in the courtyard were decorated with Catalina tiles, originals, which can retail for $100 each today.

All of the interiors had wood-beamed ceilings, intricately tiled kitchens and bathrooms, and were filled with light from a variety of sources: huge windows overlooking the courtyard, clerestory windows and, especially effective (and difficult and expensive to replicate these days), lunette windows in the upper part of several living rooms. All of the apartments boasted impressive Italian Renaissance-style fireplaces of cast concrete, some of which stand six feet tall. The place even had a hitching post alongside the still unpaved Franklin Avenue, where Zwebell would occasionally tie up his horse.

The romantic ambiance achieved by centering the apartments—more like adjoining townhouses than apartments—around a courtyard with a large fountain was popular with the film community from the start, and, today, people employed in the film industry make up the majority of the tenants. But since it is very difficult to authenticate

Opposite: Hallmarks of architect Arthur Zwebell's design for the building are twenty-foot ceilings and Italianate-style cast concrete fireplaces, which are common to most units.

Most of the apartments are on two levels, and many of the stair risers are fronted with now-rare Catalina tiles.

residence in rental property (few records remain), it's hard to know who actually lived there. When Franklin Avenue was widened on its north side, sometime in the 1940s, the entrance of the building was moved to a side-street frontage causing the renumbering of all the addresses. That made tracking down records of earlier tenancies an impossibility. One of the Talmadge sisters may have lived in one of the apartments, and F. Scott Fitzgerald may have been a resident for a time. But, despite claims in a number of publications, Rudolph Valentino could neither have lived there nor used it as a film set; the "Latin Lover" died in 1926, a year before the building was erected.

Hollywood started going downhill in the late 1960s. As drug and crime problems increased in the area, more and more of the El Cabrillo's apartments became empty. Someone painted the entire building pea green. Vagrants camped out in empty apartments, burning many of the original doors in the spectacular fireplaces to keep warm.

A savior arrived who bought the building and was determined to restore it. The vagrants were removed, doors were replaced with ones matching the originals, and that pea-green paint was sandblasted, returning the exterior of the building to its original appearance. Unfortunately, some of the restoration was not as well informed as it should have been; the sandblasting was also done on some of the interior beams and columns, leaving their surfaces pitted and rough.

The kitchens are a perfect example of the problems of bringing a golden-age building through the decades. Some of them still resemble the originals, and lack the number of electric outlets needed in a modern kitchen (although the original built-in iceboxes have been replaced by small refrigerators). Some have disposals and dishwashers. One of the kitchens was restored sometime in the 1960s, color-coordinated in the era's notorious "avocado" hue, another in the same decade's "harvest gold" color. Although all of the kitchens were originally floored with linoleum (1920s reproduction linoleum is readily available), many have been paved with cheap tile.

The next owners, the historically informed Donna Morris and Robert Grumbles, continued much unfinished restoration, removing sheet rock that hid the beamed ceilings of several apartments and covered many of the original built-in bookshelves.

View of the living room from
the balcony of the second-level
bedroom.

Opposite: The courtyard of
the El Cabrillo apartments by
night. It's no surprise that several
movies have been made in this
romantic setting.

One kitchen was completely gutted and redone in a Spanish style more appropriate
to the building's design than to the era in which it was built. Wood floors were
refinished, earthquake damage repaired, roof tiles replaced, and the wooden
balcony over the courtyard and much of the exterior wood trim was renovated. All of
the original cast iron plumbing was replaced with copper, and the landscaping of the
courtyard was redone, turning it into a lush paradise, filled with blooming camellia
trees, several varieties of palm, roses, and a stately avocado tree. The fountain was
modernized and is one of the few Hollywood courtyard fountains still in working order.

With newer apartments equipped to better serve today's lifestyles, tenants are
clamoring for a chance to live in such romantic splendor. And the stories keep coming.
One day in the early 1990s, the owners cleaned out a storeroom in the building's
cellar and came across a cache of clothing. They put it in the courtyard with a note
that tenants could take whatever they wanted before throwing it away. Later it turned
out that, among the items unclaimed and thrown in the trash, were worn-looking boots
and a leather jacket worn by Marlon Brando in *The Wild Ones*. They had been taken
from M.G.M. by a tenant, then an employee of the studio, when he learned it was
getting rid of them. He also took one of several pairs of the ruby-red slippers worn
by Judy Garland in *The Wizard of Oz* and displayed them in his apartment at the
El Cabrillo.

A recent visit to the place was somewhat discouraging. Under a new owner, it still
has charm, but the edges are fraying. The courtyard has been relandscaped and now
resembles an uneasy compromise between desert and jungle. Because repairing the
eighty-year-old bronze door latches is expensive, an old, non-working latch was simply replaced with a modern appliance; to install it, part of the original door detailing
was ripped off—and left that way. The paint on the wood window and door framing
is in terrible shape. The decline is probably inevitable. It takes a big-hearted person to
maintain a place that is no longer commercially viable despite its historic credentials.
Recently plans were announced to convert the entire structure into condominiums, so
perhaps the final chapter on the El Cabrillo apartments has yet to be written.

ElCapitanTheatre

Opposite: Built in 1926, Hollywood's famous El Capitan Theatre was restored to its golden-age glory in 1991 by the Walt Disney Company, its present owner.

Lobby of the El Capitan.

The famous film exhibitor Marcus Loew once said: "I sell tickets to movie theaters, not to movies." He knew his public. For many moviegoers of the 1920s and 1930s, the theaters themselves where as much an escape as the films they showed. The era of the movie palace started in the 1920s, the boom decade, when every man believed he could be a king. The theaters were indeed palatial, often sheathed in gold leaf, rich fabrics, and ornate detailing. Some offered more than films; decor that evoked Egypt, Asia, or Ruritania; concerts on the mighty Wurlitzer organ (which was introduced to accompany silent films; sound would not arrive until the end of the decade); and beauty and talent contests. Since Hollywood inspired this escapism, it stands to reason that the greatest examples of the movie palace were located there. One of the grandest was the El Capitan Theatre.

By the early 1920s, Hollywood was no longer a tiny village filled with vineyards and citrus groves. Its population was close to

Hundreds of thousands of
film fans bought tickets at the
El Capitan's box office to
enter one of the grandest of
Hollywood's movie palaces.

40,000, Prospect Avenue had been paved (its name changed to Hollywood Boulevard), and the venerable Hollywood Hotel had become a social center. Real estate developer Charles Toberman, often called the "Father of Hollywood," decided to establish a thriving theater district that would shift the area's entertainment center westward from downtown Los Angeles.

In association with the now-legendary impresario Sid Grauman (who had built downtown Los Angeles's still-standing Million Dollar Theater, the most elaborate theater in America when it opened in 1918), Toberman built three exotically themed theaters: the Egyptian in 1922 (inspired by the discovery of Tutankhamen's tomb), the El Capitan in 1926, and the Chinese in 1927. That year he also built the Hollywood Roosevelt Hotel, site of the first Academy Awards in 1929, and another of the thirty-six buildings he was to erect in the film capital.

Grauman's movie palaces were used by the studios to showcase their premieres. All presented stage shows called "Grauman's Prologues" before the movie, a practice pioneered by him.

In its early days, the El Capitan was more famous as a live theater venue than as a movie palace. It opened May 3, 1926 with the play *Charlot's Revue* (starring Gertrude Lawrence and Beatrice Lilly), and more than 120 plays would be presented during the following decade, including musicals like Vincent Youmans *No, No, Nanette*, and Cole Porter's *Anything Goes*, and plays like Eugene O'Neill's only comedy, *Ah, Wilderness*. Casts included many of Hollywood's stars including Will Rogers, Clark Gable, and Joan Fontaine. But film would make the El Capitan's fame, especially *Citizen Kane*, which premiered at the theater May 1, 1941, despite the violent opposition of the powerful publisher William Randolph Hearst.

The El Capitan was designed by the architectural firm of Morgan, Walls & Clements in the Spanish Baroque Revival style. It was an eclectic firm that also designed Malibu's Adamson House, the Wiltern Theater (one of Los Angeles's

Another view of the lobby showing its fanciful Art Deco mural.

The restored auditorium of the El Capitan Theatre with its restored "Mightiest of the mighty Wurlitzer's" theater organ, front and center.

greatest Art-Deco creations), the Mayan Theater, and the Samson Tire plant in East Los Angeles (now a shopping mall), which was dressed to resemble an eighth-century B.C. Assyrian palace.

The architects would not have minded that G. Albert Lansburgh, another popular architect of the time, designed the interior of the theater in something that could be called East Indian Revival style. Everything cost $800,000, and, despite clashing design concepts, it worked then, and it still does. However, immediately after the screening of *Citizen Kane*, the theater closed for a year, during which it was remodeled as a sleek, new Moderne movie house and renamed the Hollywood Paramount.

In 1989, The Walt Disney Company joined forces with Pacific Theaters to begin a two-year archaeological dig, which led to a museum-quality restoration of the legendary palace. Under the supervision of the National Park Service's Department of the Interior, and with guidance from conservationist Martin Weil, architect Eddie Fields, and theater designer Joseph J. Musil, the certified national historic site was restored in 1991 to its former grandeur. It reopened to the public as a first-run theater for Walt Disney Pictures, Walt Disney Studios, and Buena Vista Pictures Distribution, with the world premiere of Walt Disney Pictures's *The Rocketeer*.

True to the ambiance of a historic movie palace, a famous Wurlitzer organ—originally installed in 1929 in San Francisco's Fox Theater—was acquired, restored over a one-year period, and installed in the El Capitan. The last of five huge "Fox Special's" built in the 1920s, it was designed with all the bells and whistles for a movie palace, including four keyboards and 2,500 pipes installed on chambers on each side of the auditorium—the largest pipe being more than thirty-two feet long. Like the El Capitan itself, this "Mightiest of Mighty Wurlitzers" has come to life in its restored, original form. Together they are again providing filmgoers an experience from Hollywood's golden age.

Grauman's Chinese Theater

Opposite: Auditorium of what is probably the most famous movie palace in the world—Grauman's Chinese Theater.

Beginning in 1927, when the theater opened, hundreds of stars (and at least one horse) have left their imprints in cement.

Just as the El Capitan Theatre is a time machine to an era when moviegoing was the ultimate entertainment, a visit to the Chinese Theater across the street is a trip to a Hollywood fantasyland. It has been called the most famous theater in the world. It is a stone and plaster avatar of the exotic escapism at its most exuberant. Since its opening on May 18, 1927, it has been the site of more gala movie premieres than any other theater. And it is the one place in the film capital where many of the most glamorous stars in history left tangible reminders of their presence.

"America's Sweetheart" Mary Pickford, Marilyn Monroe, Paul Newman, hundreds of other film stars, a few other celebrities, and even some animals like Roy Rogers's horse, Trigger, have left their footprints, handprints, and signatures in cement in the theater's forecourt. (Some 250 are on display; the rest are stored for lack of space.) It is estimated that more than a billion visitors have tried to fit their hands or feet into these physical reminders. Many fans of the

The fantasy facade of Grauman's Chinese Theater, the most popular tourist destination in Hollywood for more than three-quarters of a century.

I Love Lucy television show still remember the episode filmed at the Chinese Theater in which Lucy steals the cement block bearing John Wayne's footprints as a souvenir. And, in a memorable *Beverly Hillbillies* episode, Jed and Jethro, thinking that the forecourt had been vandalized by stars, are caught trying to pave over the "evidence" with wet cement.

Besides hosting three Academy Awards ceremonies in the 1940s, Grauman's Chinese costarred in many movies, including the original *A Star Is Born*, and the opening scene of the 1952 musical *Singing in the Rain*. More recently, it was featured in the climax of the action-adventure film *Speed*, and in the 1998 remake of *Mighty Joe Young*, in which a gorilla climbs up the side of the theater and perches on the roof.

The theater was designed by the architectural firm of Meyer & Holler, who had previously designed the Egyptian Theater for Grauman and his partners, who included C.E. Toberman and Joseph Schenck (president of United Artists Studio). Architect Raymond Kennedy, who designed the building with D.R. Wilkerson and John Beckman, explained that the style chosen for the new theater was not traditional Chinese architecture, which was felt to be too heavy, but the more delicate eighteenth-century interpretation by Chippendale.

The ornate jade green and bronze roof, resembling a giant pagoda with silhouettes of tiny dragons running up and down its sides, has defined the Hollywood skyline for decades. Other Asian details of the theater's facade include a huge dragon, which snakes its way between the coral red columns (topped by iron masks) that architecturally support the roof, and two authentic Ming-Dynasty stone heaven-dogs that guard the main entrance.

The lobby, renovated and enlarged in 2001, is lit by a colossal chandelier—a giant replica of an incense burner. Around the walls and framed by gleaming gold and red columns, murals depict life in the Orient. The carpeting is bright red with a huge dragon in the center. A few years ago, a glass case in the west wing of the

lobby held three figures wearing authentic Chinese costumes (like those worn by the usherettes when the theater opened). The figures were grouped around a chair in which a wax image of actress Rhonda Fleming sat. She was the wife of producer and theater entrepreneur Ted Mann, who in 1973 bought the theater chain that included the Chinese. Mann sold it in 1986, and Fleming was thrown out some time later.

Inside the auditorium, a huge chandelier replicating a Chinese lantern is centered on an elaborate gold starburst on the ceiling. The starburst is in turn surrounded by a ring of dragons and an outer ring of icons depicting scenes from Chinese drama. Smaller oriental-style lamps glow at the sides of the auditorium, hanging between intricately carved stone columns and murals of trees and pagodas. The carpet is bright red, as is the upholstery on the 1,162 seats. On a balcony, there are four large boxes for visiting celebrities, and, throughout the theater, a large number of assorted oriental vases, shields, and gongs.

Most visitors have found all this impressive and beautiful. But not Pittsburgh playboy Harry K. Thaw who, in 1906, killed Stanford White, one of America's most famous architects, in a jealous rage over the professional beauty Evelyn Nesbitt. (Thaw was subsequently acquitted as being temporarily insane at the time, and married Nesbitt.) On a visit to the Chinese Theater, he reportedly took one look, clasped his hands to his head, and exclaimed: "My God! I shot the wrong architect!"

After an immensely successful premiere in New York City, Cecil B. DeMille's *King of Kings* was the opening film at the Chinese Theater. Nearly 100,000 spectators jammed Hollywood Boulevard outside the theater as stars arrived. D.W. Griffith was the master of ceremonies and Mary Pickford, then the most popular star in the world, pushed a jade button that opened the theater's curtain. It was a long night. In all his theaters, Grauman preceded his movies with stage shows, and the biblically-themed prologue extended the evening until 2 A.M.

Pickford and her husband, Doug Fairbanks, as well as Sid Grauman each owned an interest in the Chinese Theater, one of three built by Toberman and Grauman (the others were the El Capitan and the earlier Egyptian Theater, now headquarters of the American Cinemateque). Pickford's participation offers one theory as to how the idea of having stars leave their imprints in the forecourt came about. Some say it all started when Grauman accidentally stepped in fresh cement while walking across the forecourt of his new theater. Others think it was DeMille's idea. But many believe it was Pickford, who brought a tightfisted shrewdness to everything she did and, after all, had a financial interest in the theater. There is no dispute that Grauman, Norma Talmadge, Fairbanks, and Pickford made the first imprints; Talmadge, in fact, wrote the date of the grand opening of the theater above her signature instead of the date she actually made the impressions.

As the City of Los Angeles Heritage Board stated when declaring the theater an Historic-Cultural Monument in 1968: "Grauman's Chinese Theater is an example of an era in Hollywood that will never be surpassed. It is the zenith of exotic architecture, familiar to millions the world over."

Opposite: Another view of the auditorium, where more gala premieres have been held than in any other theater in Hollywood.

HaleyResidence

Opposite: A large outdoor gazebo is a favorite party site at actor and designer Kevin Haley's home. A true hidden treasure, this peaceful setting is only one block off busy Hollywood Boulevard.

Set amid lush tropical foliage, the ambiance of Haley's home, restored in 1997–2000, is more Hawaiian than Hollywood.

In 1915, while scouting for a hilltop home in Hollywood, the great actor John Barrymore remarked of the barren, sagebrush-covered landscape: "My God, almost anything we do here will be an improvement."

Although there were (and still are) some bleak vistas in and around the hills of Hollywood then, Barrymore was being unfair. Just off Hollywood Boulevard, a small enclave of charming homes was creeping its way up the side of one of the hills. One such home is said to have been the place where Edgar Rice Burroughs lived when he wrote the first of his Tarzan books. Another urban myth; Burroughs was in Chicago when he wrote *Tarzan of the Apes* and, after moving to Southern California, lived in a number of places—but not this house—before ending up on his Tarzana Ranch in the San Fernando Valley. However, across the street, and reached by a narrow stair that seems to climb straight up the side of the hill is a place that is really special.

Opposite: French doors
surrounding the living room
remind one that the house was
built long before air conditioning
came into general use.

The veranda off the living and
dining rooms is sheltered by a
bamboo forest.

The house isn't known for once being the home of a famous star, although it was the location for *Surrender*, a romantic comedy made in 1987 starring Michael Caine and Sally Field. Nor is it known for anything historic taking place under its roof. And it isn't the oldest house in Hollywood, though, as it was built in 1921, it is one of the oldest remaining. With 2,000 square feet and two bedrooms, it is a small house by Hollywood standards and cost only $3,000, about the average at the time. But everyone who visits the house today, owned since 1997 by actor turned interior designer Kevin Haley, agrees that it is the prettiest and most charming home in the film capital.

One reason is its setting, hidden in a thick tropical jungle of bamboo, palm, and palmetto. Hollywood Boulevard does not intrude, nor does Los Angeles itself. Another reason is the home's idyllic appearance, unaltered from a time when there was no television, air-conditioning, computers, nor much of the technology we take for granted today. The house evokes a turn-of-the-century plantation in Hawaii rather than a busy urban setting. But, unlike some of the houses in this book, this one isn't an escapist fantasy; it was built by an architect for his family to live in. The whimsical aspect of the house has evolved with decades of lifestyle changes and Haley's imaginative decorating decisions.

Not much is known about the man who built this house other than that he was an architect named Jacques Serdoulf. Before it was built, a previous house on the property had to be demolished, making the place one of the earliest examples of a "tear-down" property, now popular among leaders in the film community. It is constructed of lath and stucco with redwood girders and studs. "It was the first and only house I looked at when I bought it," Haley recalls. "You could hardly see the house at all then," he adds. "Now you can't see it at all."

Chinese scenes painted on silk cover the dining room walls.

Opposite: The centerpiece of Haley's skylit period kitchen is a restored, classic O'Keefe & Merrit range, which is enameled robins-egg blue.

Although the house wasn't falling apart, it certainly wasn't in good condition. "It was visually horrible," Haley says. One of the first things he did was to rebuild the stairs and walkway leading up to the house with antique brick imported from England; another was to replace the various retaining walls on the property with walls of stone quarried from the hill behind the house. Halfway up the hill from the street, the designer built a large outdoor gazebo—measuring 20 × 25 feet, it is more like an outdoor living room. It is furnished with tables, sofa, and chairs, and even boasts an outdoor shower.

Inside the house, Haley resurfaced everything. Carpeting was removed from the floors and the wood was refinished and stained dark. The hipped plaster ceiling in the living room was finished with an ivory-toned wax; the room's mantle and all of the trim downstairs was painted a turquoise hue matching the 1960s chandelier Haley discovered and hung in the dining room, whose walls are covered with hand-painted Chinese-themed murals of silk. Around the dining table (designed by Haley), are chairs by the Finnish architect Alvar Aalto, which were stained and upholstered in white leather in the 1960s by Hollywood decorator William Haines.

There are a number of pieces in the house that were designed by Haines, a popular film star in 1920s whose life proved that living well is the best revenge. After Haines was fired by the homophobic Louis B. Mayer, when he was caught *in flagrante delicto* with a young sailor, Haines's Hollywood friends, among whom were Joan Crawford and Carole Lombard, immediately hired him to decorate their homes. Years later, the multimillionaire decorator capped a hugely successful career by redecorating the American embassy in London when publisher Walter Annenberg was ambassador.

Left: Lucite and black mirror nightstands designed by Haley flank the bed in the small master bedroom.

The master bath is sheathed in blue glass mosaic tiles.

The sense of being in another place is especially strong in the home's high-ceilinged living room, where, for cooling, French doors open wide onto a broad veranda on the room's southern and eastern exposures. The sofa was designed by Haley; the glass, Lucite, and brass coffee table is Italian and dates from the 1960s; and the Steinway piano in the corner was manufactured in 1919. One of the unusual design elements in a house this small is the double-stair opening onto the living room, and here Haley imposed what is perhaps the most striking of his design choices: a wall lacquered lipstick red. It is flanked by smoked glass mirrors in front of which are a pair of antique Chinese cabinets. In the master bedroom, on either side of the bed are Lucite and black mirror night stands (also designed by Haley), and the guest room/study hides the only obvious bow to technology in the house—a giant television screen and stereo equipment. Back downstairs, the kitchen is highlighted by an old O'Keefe and Merritt range, which Haley rechromed and reenameled in a sky blue color; outside is a seven-foot-deep plunge pool and Jacuzzi installed by the owner.

"For me," Haley muses, "I get a sense of peace the second I walk up to the house. I feel protected and safe here." Few residences succeed in providing this feeling as this small house in the Hollywood Hills.

Outside the kitchen entrance, Haley installed a tiny seven-foot-deep pool and Jacuzzi.

HolidayHouse Motel

Opposite: Originally designed in 1948 as a Malibu motel by the celebrated architect Richard Neutra, this building was renovated as ocean-view condominiums in 1979 and largely restored in 1993.

The kidney-shaped pool of Neutra's motel, where John Fitzgerald Kennedy is said to have romanced Marilyn Monroe during the Los Angeles 1960 Democratic convention.

As mentioned earlier, Richard Neutra was one of the most prolific and celebrated of the high-art modernist architects of the past mid-century. In the early 1920s, the Vienna-born architect Rudolph Schindler, then supervising the construction of Frank Lloyd Wright's "Hollyhock House," wrote his friend Richard Neutra, who was still in Austria. "Come to Los Angeles," he commanded. "They're building a new city here." Eventually he and his wife, Dione, arrived, having been prompted by a poster they saw while visiting Zurich, Switzerland, that read "California Calls You!"

Neutra and Schindler would spend the rest of their lives creating homes and buildings that would—along with Frank Lloyd Wright—revolutionize architecture in America. At first, Neutra wasn't comfortable with the locals, finding them "mentally footloose." Nevertheless, because of a philosophical outlook that welcomed the non-traditional, the warm climate, and the availability of money (his houses were very expensive for the time), Neutra came to love Los Angeles. It

The efficient kitchen in the unit owned by Paul Wright. The living room is to the right.

was a place that allowed him to design structures where indoor and outdoor spaces flowed together, to realize a desire to "place man in relationship with nature; that's where he developed and where he feels most at home."

Neutra's first house in Hollywood is probably his most famous: the Lovell House (see image pp. 10–11 of the Preface), built in the Hollywood Hills in 1929 for Dr. Philip Lovell, the *Los Angeles Times* health and fitness columnist. It cost $50,000 to build, a tremendous amount for the time, but it has been treasured by subsequent tenants. It was also featured in the film *L.A. Confidential,* where it served as the home of Pierce Patchett, the man who ran a ring of prostitutes who were meticulously dressed and made up to resemble famous movie stars.

Many Neutra designs have been lost, are poorly maintained, or have been modified beyond recognition. Such is the case of the restaurant for the Holiday House motel complex he designed in 1948 atop an eighty-foot bluff beside the ocean in Malibu; renamed Geoffrey's, it bears little resemblance to Neutra's concept. Although the complex's original eighteen motel rooms were turned into townhouses in 1979 and subsequently modified into eight condominiums (a concrete retaining wall was also added after the 1993 earthquake), it looks much as it did when it was promoted as being "only fifty minutes from downtown but a million miles away." Stars loved it, especially Bette Davis who is said to have stayed there often. John Kennedy and Marilyn Monroe liked it as well; they reportedly enjoyed a tryst there during the 1960 Democratic convention.

The condos are small for a full-time home; only 700 square feet. But the fact that residents choose to make these their primary homes says everything about the ingenuity of Neutra's concept. Consider the ocean view beyond the large deck and

Opposite: The condominiums, converted from hotel rooms, may be small, but the patios (and views) are huge.

Above: Paul Wright's Neutra-designed skylit bathroom.

The sleeping area.

Opposite: Paul Wright's Asian-themed living room and sleeping area. His flat screen television, bathroom—with its curved wall and glass brick interior window— and the kitchen beyond are reflected in the mirror behind the sofa.

the kidney shaped pool: framed in the architect's floor-to-ceiling windows, it spans a vast space from the Palos Verdes Peninsula to the Channel Islands. "I have a July 4 party every year," says resident Paul Wright, a lawyer with a Malibu practice who is also president of the British-American Business Council of Los Angeles and head of the homeowner's association. "The sight is amazing. Several Malibuites also organize fireworks displays from barges anchored in front of their beach homes which seem to explode right in front of my place."

The view and the fireworks aren't the main reasons for Wright's happiness with his home, which he bought in 1999. The use of space contained within the twelve-foot, skylighted ceilings gives him the most satisfaction. "I love Neutra's style," he says. "And the omnipresence of nature. I work very hard, and, when I come home, I want an uncluttered ambiance to clear my mind. This place is perfect. It has a sort of Japanese minimalist feel to it. " To make the small space work for him, Wright made a few modifications, including a ten-foot curved beechwood credenza and a Japanese screen to isolate the bedroom area. He also removed the marble fireplace facing added by the previous owner, and built out the fireplace four inches to sink a flat-screen television above it. Otherwise, all he did was "spruce it up" a bit. "I feel blessed to be there," Wright says. "It's a hidden gem; a little piece of heaven."

MaxFactorBuilding

Opposite: Max Factor's showcase building was restored, over a seven year period in the 1990s, as the Hollywood History Museum.

Bette Davis and Max Factor in the early 1930s.

Qualification for stardom has always been based on an actor's looks. As Marilyn Monroe once recalled: "In Hollywood a girl's virtue is much less important than her hairdo. You're judged by how you look, not by what you are." However more than natural beauty is needed to look terrific on screen. Enter the makeup artist.

In the early days of film the makeup artist's job was less that of making a star look great than of helping him or her survive the transition from live action onto the very slow and primitive orthochromatic film used at the time. The stark makeup necessary to convey an image would melt under the hot glare of the klieg lights and need to be redone often in the course of filming a scene. The film was also insensitive to blue, so blue eyes would photograph blank. Cecil B. DeMille partially solved the problem by having an assistant hold a strip of black velvet near the camera. When the actors looked at it, their eyes dilated and, at least, the pupils would photograph. With panchromatic film, introduced in the mid-1920s, matters improved

Opposite: The Max Factor
building (top) and the ornate
lobby in 1938.

The original green marble
entrance of Max Factor's
exuberantly Art Deco makeup
palace.

dramatically and makeup became more natural. By then, the man who would become the most famous makeup artist in Hollywood and the father of a makeup empire that endures to this day, was already on his way.

Born in Lodz, Poland, in 1877, Max Factor, one of ten children, was apprenticed at the age of eight to a dentist-pharmacist. After serving in the Russian army, where he used his pharmacological background to concoct skin-colored creams to hide combat scars, Factor opened a shop in a Moscow suburb where he sold handmade rouges, creams, fragrances, wigs, and a convenient pancake makeup he invented. It would make him famous years later when he introduced it to the Hollywood film industry. One day, according to Factor's reminiscences, a traveling theatrical group wore Factor's makeup when performing for the royal family, which appointed him their official cosmetician as well as that of the Imperial Russian Grand Opera.

In 1904 he and his wife came to America to cash in on the World's Fair in St. Louis, where he sold makeup under the name of Max Factor, given to him by the inspectors at Ellis Island. In 1908 he moved his family to Los Angeles where, a decade later, he developed a "flexible-greasepaint" that wouldn't crack or cake; the industry immediately seized upon it. He also went into the wig business. Because wigs were expensive, he rented them on the condition that his sons be cast in the movies in which they were used to keep an eye on the wigs. All three of his sons can be spotted as extras in Cecil B. DeMille's first movie, *The Squaw Man,* made in 1913. In addition to introducing his trademark pancake makeup to Hollywood, he created a new language for cosmetics, which included false eyelashes, the eyebrow pencil, and lip gloss.

Another view of the lobby
in 1938.

In 1928, Factor created a palatial building across the street from the Hollywood Hotel, situated where the Hollywood and Highland complex stands today. It became a focal point in the film capital, attracting both movie people and, after 1927, much of L.A. society, when he started selling his cosmetics to the non-film consumers. In his palace of pancake, Factor surrounded his illustrious clients with movielike splendor, furnishing his street-level public rooms with crystal chandeliers, gold sconces, parquet and marble floors, and display cabinets styled as Louis XVI furniture. In 1934, Factor hired a famous theater architect, S. Charles Lee (among his works is the Bruin Theater in L.A.'s Westwood community), to transform the facade of his building into an Art Deco fantasy, highlighted with green marble columns and pilasters.

One secret of Factor's success is that he innately understood the right color matches for his clients, and the results—like Joan Crawford's blood-red slash of a mouth or Bette Davis's emphatically made-up eyes—would often define a star's "look." In his new building Factor designed several rooms specially painted to enable such makeovers. There was a room painted a special green for redheads; in it, Lucille Ball, who had originally opted for the sultry blonde look of the era, emerged as the carrot-top which she remained for all her life. It was to this room that Columbia boss Harry Cohn brought a dark-haired discovery named Margarita Cansino, who walked out as the lustrous redhead known as Rita Hayworth. There was a two-tone blue room where stars like Jean Harlow became blondes, a peach and beige room for "brownettes" (in which Judy Garland also lost her original frumpy looks), and a dusty-pink room for brunettes. Upstairs was Factor's makeup factory. Also upstairs was a garage reached by the largest elevator in Hollywood. Stars used it to store their expensive Packards, Rolls Royces, and Duesenbergs while away on location. Downstairs, Factor installed a bowling alley and a night club.

Opposite: The restored lobby with
the original display cases. To the
left are two of the makeup rooms.

In 1938 Factor died, and although his son transformed the company into a worldwide provider of name-brand cosmetics, Max Factor's Hollywood palace slowly deteriorated, as ownership passed through a variety of corporations that didn't know what to do with it.

But Donelle Dadigan did, the Beverly Hills real estate developer who had dreamed of one day putting together a museum of Hollywood history, and the Factor building was perfect. She took seven years and $8 million to restore the Max Factor Building as the Hollywood Museum, during the 1990s and the results are worth it.

Upstairs where Factor's makeup factory was located, two floors are devoted to the display of more than 5,000 pieces of art and artifacts from Hollywood's history. Included are such rare items as Mae West's boudoir, the emperor's deathbed from the film *Gladiator,* and the dinosaur egg incubator from *Jurassic Park.* There is also a spectacular collection of historic photographs, sets, props, and costumes including gowns worn by Marilyn Monroe, Bette Davis, and Elizabeth Taylor. When the elevator is not in use carrying equipment for the many parties held in the museum, Cary Grant's vintage Rolls Royce is parked in it.

Using S. Charles Lee's original plans, Donelle Dadigan returned the first floor to its original elegance. Grimy brown carpeting has been replaced with gleaming gray Italian marble floors, the original sconces have been overhauled, and the original gilded wall moldings replicated. Some of the original makeup cases (as well as makeup, still in its containers) and Factor's personal makeup chair were discovered and restored. Crucial to the original design was the color of the paints used in the makeover rooms; luckily the Dunn Edwards Paint Company paint charts were found and the company mixed the paint colors to the original formulas. There are few places in Hollywood or anywhere else where a visitor can walk through a door and be instantly transported back in time to a more glamorous era. The Hollywood Museum is one of those places.

Many stars once stored their cars on the top floor of the building. It was reached by what is still the largest elevator in Hollywood, off which this 1960 Rolls Royce, once owned by Cary Grant, is being driven.

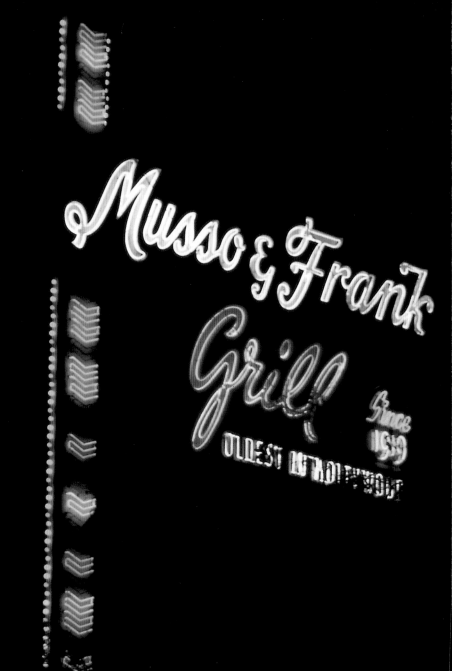

Musso & Frank
Grill
Since
1919
OLDEST IN HOLLYWOOD

OLDEST RESTAURANT IN HOLLYWOOD
SINCE 1919

Musso&Frank Grill

Opposite: The Musso & Frank Grill, the oldest restaurant in Hollywood. The restaurant has been enlarged and restored several times over the years, most recently in the mid-1950s.

The restaurant in 1944.

"You're in Raymond Chandler territory," said one review of Musso & Frank Grill, Hollywood's oldest restaurant. The reviewer was wrong. Chandler was a noir writer of mean streets and mean people, and there is nothing noir about Musso's. A visit to Musso's is more like a trip to F. Scott Fitzgerald territory—the right bonhomie, the right food, and the best martini in town. Fitzgerald was a regular when he was toiling in Hollywood as a screenwriter.

From the day it opened in 1919, Musso & Frank Grill was a hit with both stars and working stiffs. Founded by Frank Toulet and John Musso, who owned the place for six years, in 1936 it was relocated by new owners to larger quarters next door to its original Hollywood Boulevard location. In the mid-1950s it was expanded again with the addition of a large room in the space next door, formerly occupied by the famous Stanley Rose bookstore. This explains Musso's popularity—at least during Hollywood's golden age—with writers as well as stars. Many high-profile writers hung out in Rose's

The menu, virtually unchanged since 1922, features all-American standards like meat loaf, corned beef and, still a favorite, Chicken à la King.

Opposite: Over the years, stars—including Charles Chaplin, John Barrymore, Tom Selleck, and Julia Roberts—have felt at home here.

bookstore (which boasted slot machines in the back), among them John O'Hara, Erskine Caldwell, Dashiell Hammett, John Steinbeck, Gene Fowler, and William Faulkner. It was convenient to stop in next door for some liquid refreshment (Faulkner would mix his own mint juleps) and, perhaps, a meal. Rose himself was a self-proclaimed con-man and an intimate of many local drug dealers, gangsters, and pimps. Memorialized by Nathanael West in his novel *The Day of the Locust* (Rose's name is mentioned as an endorsement on the business card of a shady character named Honest Abe Kusich), the bookstore owner later became a literary agent representing, among others, William Saroyan.

But it was the stars and not the writers who popularized Musso's. Charlie Chaplin was a regular who always sat at table number 1 (often with wife Paulette Goddard) so he could watch the boulevard while sipping his martini. On one occasion he provided the spectacle; in the early 1920s, Chaplin and John Barrymore decided to have a horse race down Hollywood Boulevard; the loser was to buy dinner at Musso & Frank. The parking lot behind Musso's once boasted horse stalls; today patrons in the know enter the restaurant through the parking lot door—never the front door.

Other regulars include the Marx Brothers, Clark Gable, John Gilbert, Gilbert Roland, Humphrey Bogart, Jack Webb, Raymond Burr, Marlene Dietrich (who also hung out at the Rose bookstore), and Ralph Edwards. Steve McQueen always sat on stool number 1 at the counter; after McQueen's death, the late character actor Alan Hale Jr. (from *Gilligan's Island*) claimed the stool. Today the restaurant's famous flannel cake is a favorite of Julia Roberts. Tom Selleck is said to prefer table 24; Al Pacino, table 28.

One reason for the popularity of the restaurant is the menu, largely unchanged
from 1922 when Jean Leon Rue, schooled in Paris, was chef. The food is basic
old-style American, untouched by innovations like California cuisine. Among the most
popular items on the menu are corned beef, short ribs, broiled chicken, and chicken
à la king. The present chef, Michel Bourger, has retained Chef Rue's original recipes.
So what has changed? Certainly not the waiters who famously remain at their stations
for decades.

One of the veteran waiters, Manuel Felix, joined the restaurant in 1973. "The
biggest change," he says, "is dress. People used to come dressed up; now they come
anyway they want [the restaurant does enforce a no-tank-top dress code]. Broiled
chicken used to be $5.25," he laughs. "Now it is $17.50."

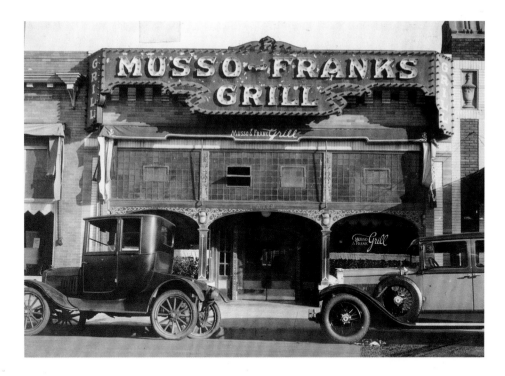

Pig'N'Whistle Restaurant

Opposite: The famous Pig 'N' Whistle, which opened as Hollywood's first family-style restaurant in 1927, was restored in 1999.

The restaurant in 1944.

By 1927 the popularity of the movies had created celebrities. Mary Pickford's husband, Doug Fairbanks, was one of the most popular male stars in the world through his roles in swashbucklers like *The Thief of Bagdad*, *The Black Pirate*, and *Robin Hood*, the most expensive movie ever made until *Gone With the Wind* came along seventeen years later. He wasn't the most famous male actor; that title belonged to Charlie Chaplin and, until his death the year before, Rudolph Valentino.

Hollywood Boulevard had been paved a few years earlier, but a trolley still ran down its center, disgorging its passengers at the stop in front of the Hollywood Hotel. Sid Grauman's Chinese Theater was next door to the hotel. Down the street was the Roosevelt Hotel, which two years later would host the first Academy Awards ceremony.

The hungry visitor might head to the brand new Pig 'N' Whistle restaurant. It joined Grauman's first Hollywood theater, the Egyptian,

The doors of the Pig 'N' Whistle have welcomed stars and tourists alike.

which, five years earlier, had hosted the first gala movie premiere for the opening of Doug Fairbanks's *Robin Hood*.

In those days, movie houses didn't have concession counters inside their lobbies. So an entrepreneur named Stan Hoedemaker took advantage of the opportunity and, on July 22, 1927, opened Hollywood's first family restaurant and soda fountain off the courtyard of the Egyptian, where moviegoers could have a meal or a snack. He named it the Pig 'N' Whistle after the fanciful design of a dancing pig playing a flute, rediscovered on one of the original soda fountain tiles during restoration of the Egyptian Theater. Featured in a 1928 issue of *Architectural Digest*, the restaurant was designed by Morgan, Walls & Clements—the same architectural firm that designed the El Capitan—in a Gothic style of ornately carved dark wood, heavy beams, and stained glass windows. From the day it opened until the late 1940s, the restaurant thrived, surviving the Great Depression and World War II.

Shirley Temple was a regular—she loved the sodas at the soda bar up front where, today, a bar dispenses alcoholic refreshments. Spencer Tracy, Howard Hughes, and Barbara Stanwyck were regulars; Loretta Young, a devout Catholic, dined there every Sunday following church services. A 1939 issue of *Film Fan* reports that Judy Garland entertained friends at the place in the middle of making *The Wizard of Oz*. Many guests enjoyed the popular tunes played on an organ at the front of the restaurant. And every Friday night the Hollywood Glee Club would perform.

Dining family style in the 1940s.

Opposite: The restaurant's ornate interior today.

The bar was originally a soda fountain, where child stars like Shirley Temple would entertain their friends.

In 1949, business declined and the Pig 'N' Whistle closed. Over the next fifty years, the property passed from owner to owner, ending up as a seedy fast-food joint; its remarkable interior hidden beneath a dropped ceiling and false walls. But it wasn't forgotten. In 1974, Robert Towne made a reference to the restaurant in his evocation of a long-lost Hollywood in his Oscar™-winning script for *Chinatown*. "This?" asks J. J. "Jake" Gittes (Jack Nicholson) looking at a photograph of Hollis Mulwray, a Water Department engineer, and Noah Cross (John Huston) a multimillionaire seeking to pull off a water diversion scheme. P. I. Lawrence Walsh explains: "They got in a terrific argument outside the Pig 'N' Whistle."

In 1999, new owners began a $1.5 million restoration of the restaurant, ripping out the additions of later years and using old photographs of the place to reconstruct the interior. It reopened in March of 2001, with former child star Margaret O'Brien in attendance. At the same time, others were restoring the neighboring Egyptian Theater.

Today, apart from the presence of a few television sets, it is easy for a visitor to recapture the ambiance of 1927 when hungry patrons clamored for tables. Diners can enjoy the coziness offered as an escape from the business of Hollywood. Now they can see the Kodak Theater across the street, part of the vast Hollywood & Highland Center, where the Academy Awards ceremonies are held today.

VillaAurora

Opposite: The Villa Aurora today. It was restored in 1991.

Marta Feuchtwanger and her novelist-husband, Lion, in the courtyard of their villa, where they would often welcome guests.

Today the Paseo Miramar neighborhood in Pacific Palisades, once the site of silent films made by movie pioneer Thomas Ince, is one of the most exclusive in the area. Boasting tremendous views from atop a high bluff, the ambiance has been compared to the French Riviera or, with some imagination, Italy's dramatic Amalfi coast. At least that was the idea when development began.

The first house, built in 1926, was a 6,700-square-foot, twenty-room Spanish Colonial Revival-style demonstration home, a joint project between the developers Arthur Weber and George Ley and the *Los Angeles Times*. It was designed to be a showcase for modern conveniences like dishwashers and electric garage door openers—there is a trash compactor in the kitchen—but it was built to show skeptical Angelenos the benefits of living far from the city's center. It was designed by an architect and engineer named Mark Daniels, who would later design Los Angeles's celebrated Bel-Air Hotel. According to a neighbor, the name "Villa Aurora" wasn't used until

Entrance courtyard of the Villa Aurora.

the 1960s, when the surrounding community decided to give itself a Mediterranean flair by assigning Spanish or Italian-sounding names to houses in the area. "Villa Aurora" was the name carved on the marble plaque given to the owners, which is now mounted beside the entrance gate of the house. The carved and painted wooden doors and ceilings with their Moorish motifs were inspired by the Cathedral of Teruel in Spain and designed by Thorwald Probst.

According to the *Los Angeles Times* (which chronicled the building's progress with weekly articles), thousands toured the place during construction and the month following its completion, after which developer Arthur Weber moved in. Seven other mansions were also built on the hill at about the same time, including one for the celebrated opera singer Amelita Galli-Curci.

Then economic and world events took charge of the house's fate. First was the Great Depression, which made living in a villa by the sea only a dream for most people. Then came World War II which, with tire and gasoline rationing, made commuting from distant Pacific Palisades difficult. In 1943, a German historical novelist, playwright, and refugee, Lion Feuchtwanger, and his wife, Marta, bought it for $9,000. Writer Thomas Mann, who lived nearby, called the place a "veritable castle by the sea." Charged with antifascism for a novel he wrote satirizing Hitler, Feuchtwanger and his wife fled to France where they lived in exile for eight years before fleeing the Nazis again in 1941, after being interned in a French detention camp. Freed through the personal intervention of President Franklin Roosevelt, they walked across the Pyrenees to Spain, then traveled to neutral Lisbon where they sailed for the United States.

The dining room of the villa
is filled with more books from
the original owner's famous
collection.

Thomas Mann lived nearby and was a frequent guest at the villa, which he once called "a veritable castle by the sea."

The Feuchtwangers were only a small part of what has been called the greatest cultural diaspora in history; a vast migration that, according to estimates, brought half of the European intellectual and creative talent—four-fifths of them German-speaking— to a fifteen-square-mile patch of California. Why Los Angeles? The appeal of climate was part of the draw, but far more compelling was the presence of earlier émigrés, and the opportunities for work at the film studios.

The relatively remote location of the Villa Aurora was no problem for Feucht-wanger; he sought solitude for his writing in his study on the top floor. (He wrote six novels before his death in 1958.) Feuchtwanger collected books, and the spacious villa saw the birth of his third and final library, which numbered some 36,000 volumes when he died. (His first library was burned by Hitler in 1933, the second left behind in France but eventually shipped to him in Los Angeles.)

Because of the number of German exiles who also lived in the area, it became known as "the Weimar of the Pacific," and the Villa Aurora was its capital. The couple hosted readings from Lion's current novel for an audience that included Berthold Brecht, Heinrich Mann, and Thomas Mann (but never when Brecht was there; Mann and Brecht disliked each other intensely), the philosopher Ludwig Marcuse, Aldous Huxley, and the writer Franz Werfel (*The Song of Bernadette*) and his wife, Alma (formerly married to composer Gustav Mahler and Bauhaus founder Walter Gropius). The group would dine on herring salad and apple strudel. Occasionally they would play darts, using as a target a picture of Adolf Hitler; pockmarked, it still hangs in the office of the director of the foundation that owns the house today. The Feuchtwangers also entertained friends at intimate teas which included Charlie and Oona Chaplin,

Opposite: The ornately tiled
master bathroom.

When the Villa Aurora was built
in 1926, it was planned as a
showcase for the latest advances
in domestic conveniences,
including a dishwasher and a
trash compactor in the kitchen.

Charles Laughton, Peter Lorre, Albert Einstein, filmmaker Jean Renoir, and modern composer Arnold Schoenberg and his wife, Gertrude (again, never with Thomas Mann, whom Schoenberg believed satirized him in his 1947 novel *Doctor Faustus*).

Following the death of her husband, Marta Feuchtwanger bequeathed the house and library to the University of Southern California with the provision that she would live there until her death. After she died in 1987 (at the age of ninety-four), concerned Germans and Angelenos formed the Friends of Villa Aurora, a group that was determined to find a way to keep the house and library intact as a cultural monument to German writers and artists who fled the Nazi persecution and settled in Los Angeles. In 1990, with the support of such illuminati as novelist Gunther Grass and former German Chancellor Willy Brandt, and the financial help of the Berlin Lottery Foundation and the German government, the group purchased the villa in 1990 for $1.9 million. As part of the deal, the rare books in the library were transferred to U.S.C., and some 22,000 volumes were left on the shelves of the house as a permanent loan from the school. Before the nonprofit Friends of Villa Aurora organization could move in, the villa's deteriorated interior and its crumbling foundation had to be upgraded. Under the direction of architect and U.S.C. faculty member Frank Dimster, it would take three years and $1.6 million more from Germany.

The principal problem was that the house was built on top of two opposing hillsides, which were sliding downward and exerting pressure on the villa's foundation.

Entrance of the Villa Aurora.

Coupled with water erosion, portions of the foundation had been dislocated, resulting in a significant difference in the elevation of one side of the house from the other. It was clear that to stabilize the building, the foundation would have to be raised and concrete caissons poured below it. But before that could be done, an elaborate system of laser beams and monitors had to be used to determine the baseline points. The building was then lifted with a combination of 5,000 "cribs" to hold the foundation, three truckloads of steel beams, and hydraulic jacks, all coordinated with a system of air-pressure hoses connected to a large compressor. Twenty-three concrete caissons were poured, reaching forty-five feet down to bedrock, and the house was lowered back onto its new foundation.

In the spirit of Villa Aurora's mission, the house continues to be a meeting place for German, European, and American artists and intellectuals, and fosters German-American exchange in the fields of literature, art, science, and politics. Today, the main focus of the activities is its artists-in-residence program, in which ten to twelve musicians, writers, filmmakers, journalists, photographers, and other creative persons are annually invited to participate. The foundation also presents a regular series of concerts, readings, screenings, and discussions. Although the main funding comes from the German Federal Foreign Office and the German State Minister for Cultural Affairs, the Villa Aurora, a nonprofit foundation, also is dependent on the generosity of private donors.

Afterword: **Neon** Nights

The Hollywood sign is considered the symbol of the film capital; an icon of entertainment and glamour that always tops the list of places visitors to Hollywood want to see. But that hasn't always been the case. The sign was erected in 1924 as an advertisement for a real estate development named Hollywoodland, and by 1939 the sign was deteriorating seriously. It was only saved from ruin in the mid-1970s through the efforts of a few civic-minded individuals and companies. Only then would it begin its ascent to universal recognition.

During Hollywood's golden age, the real symbol of Hollywood was its collection of brilliant neon signs. Writers including William Faulkner, Christopher Isherwood, and John O'Hara were entranced by the display, and many used the galaxy of neon signs as a metaphor for the film capital itself. F. Scott Fitzgerald thought of the signs as conveying the schizophrenia of Hollywood; a place that created fantasy while being anchored in fact, conjuring escapist dreams amid worldwide economic depression. They were called "glowworms in the sky," "ribbons of living flame," and "the kitsch soul of Hollywood." Raymond Chandler recalled this time in his novel *The Little Sister*: "I smelled Los Angeles before I got to it, it smelled stale and old like a living room that had been closed for too long. But

Opposite and following spreads: A few of Hollywood's historic neon signs, many of which were restored and relit in the late 1990s. The Formosa Café (opposite) served as a location in the movie *L.A. Confidential.*

the colored lights fooled you. The lights were wonderful. There ought to be a monument to the man who invented neon lights."

In 1923, Los Angeles was the first place in the United States to employ neon lighting as outdoor advertising, when the local Packard dealer and radio pioneer, Earle C. Anthony, bought three blue-and-orange signs in the Packard logo script for $24,000. He mounted one of them on the roof of his dealership at Seventh and Flower in downtown Los Angeles, another inside the dealership, and the third was on the roof of Anthony's San Francisco dealership.

The new lighting took America by storm. It was bright (about triple the brilliance of incandescent lights of the same power), cheap to operate, and colorful. And its flexibility fit right in with the growing popularity of Streamline Moderne architecture with its curves, dramatic cantilevers, and imaginative use of glass. When Chandler wrote his novel in 1949, however, those neon lights had been extinguished for seven years, and no one knew when they would ever be lit again. In February 1942, Los Angeles Mayor Fletcher Bowron, besieged by rumors of imminent Japanese air raids, had ordered all the neon signs blacked out. It would be more than fifty years before most of them were turned on again.

By the 1960s, Hollywood was beset by the popularity of television, the government-forced breakup of the studio-exhibitor monopoly, and the rising popularity of independent filmmaking. Many of its other lights were going out as residents fled the community for the San Fernando Valley and the safer, less crowded Westside of Los Angeles. Businesses vanished, to be replaced by sleazy mini malls, tattoo parlors, and cheap souvenir shops catering to tourists. Drugs arrived in force and became so serious that at least one resident of the El Cabrillo apartments (see pp. 166–73) was occasionally forced to lie on the floor to avoid being hit by bullets.

It took years, a firm police presence, and determination for Hollywood to return to its present physical grace. Today the presence of such new structures as the Hollywood & Highland Center and restored monuments like the El Capitan and Egyptian theaters creates a far more pleasant ambience. However, in the early 1990s, Adolfo Nodal, then general manager of Los Angeles's Cultural Affairs Department, realized something was missing. Inspired by Raymond Chandler's lines, he set out to raise the money to restore the old signs, both on Wilshire Boulevard and in Hollywood proper. By the end of the decade, some 125 gigantic display signs had been reborn. The lights were on again. The soul of Hollywood had been restored.

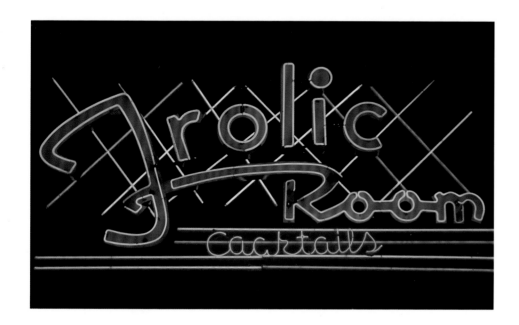

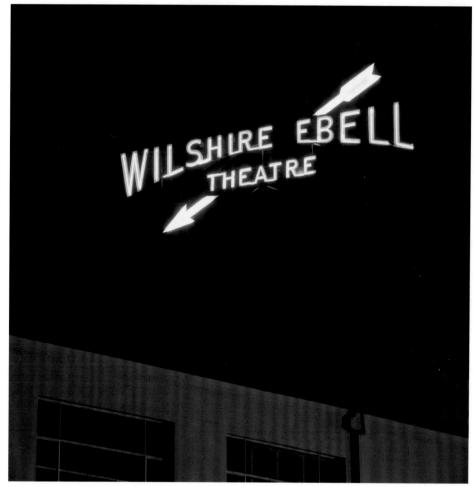

Index

Project management and principal editing: Richard Olsen
Designer: Binocular, New York
Production management: Jane Searle
Copyediting: Sigi Nacson

Library of Congress Cataloging-in-Publication Data
Wallace, David.
  Dream palaces of Hollywood's Golden Age / by David Wallace ;
photography by
Juergen Nogai.—1st ed.
      p. cm.
  Includes index.
  ISBN 0-8109-5543-1 (hardcover : alk. paper)
  1. Mansions—California—Los Angeles. 2. Historic buildings—
California—Los Angeles. 3. Architecture—California—Los Angeles-
—20th century. 4. Los Angeles (California)-Buildings, structures, etc.
5. Hollywood (Los Angeles, Calif.)—Buildings, structures, etc. I. Title.

  NA735.L55W35 2006
  728.809794'94-dc22
                    2005028031

Printed and bound in China
10 9 8 7 6 5 4 3 2 1

harry n. abrams, inc.
a subsidiary of La Martinière Groupe

115 West 18th Street
New York, NY 10011
www.hnabooks.com